Speak Money

Fulphil Publishing

979-8-9877411-8-4 (hardcover)
979-8-9896889-0-6 (paperback)
979-8-9896889-1-3 (ebook)
979-8-9896889-2-0 (audiobook)

Library of Congress Catalog Card Number: 0000-0000
Copyright © 2023 by Fulphil Publishing

Tiffany Yau (Author)
Naiomi Israel (Foreword)

DEDICATION

This book is dedicated to Naiomi Israel, Kathrina Miranda, Quency Phillips, Deryk Clark, and Vanita Lee-Tatum, some of the greatest advocates and leaders I know for creating equitable access to financial literacy.

Thank you to our friends of Fulphil, from our editors, partners, students, teachers, team, and beyond — without you, this book would not be possible.

TABLE OF CONTENTS

FOREWORD

I grew up in the culture-rich streets of Jamaica Queens, surrounded by the loud laughter and stories of my amazing, close-knit family. But I won't sugarcoat it—our living situation was far from ideal. Despite every adult working tirelessly, we relied on government assistance to provide enough food and medical services for my multigenerational Jamaican household.

My passion for economic mobility sprouted from the seeds of poverty. Growing up poor and Black, I couldn't help but notice that the whiter a neighborhood, the better its living conditions—the bigger houses, the beautiful parks, the manicured lawns. I envisioned a world where racial demographics didn't dictate property values. So, during the pandemic, I embarked on a minor in economics at NYU, and that's where Fulphil entered the picture.

I became an intern at Fulphil, and as I continued my journey there, Tiffany proposed that I help her and the team design a financial literacy curriculum. I admit, I was terrified. While financial literacy was different from economic mobility, I believed in its importance.

Tiffany's unwavering trust in me felt like a monumental responsibility for someone who had grown up with a fixed mindset as a "poor Black girl" I am grateful for our partnership and her inspiration to create this course. The research was relentless, and we created fantastic videos to accompany the course. I felt like I was living a dream, knowing that I could make a difference by helping people become more financially literate.

Then, in 2021, our financial literacy course was piloted as a summer course for people ranging from middle school students to those in middle age. The feedback we received was overwhelming but heartfelt. This course remains one of my greatest accomplishments, and it wouldn't have been possible without Tiffany, who tirelessly penned most of our chapters.

Today, I continue to follow my passion for bringing financial education to schools around the country through an organization called FiCycle, where I serve as the Program Director. Witnessing students never ask, "When will I use this?" in a math class is truly fulfilling. It's a testament to the power of the integration of financial literacy education within rigorous math courses.

Always remember, that math is your primary tool for making financial decisions, and I'm delighted that you have this book to guide you on your journey to financial wellness. My hope is that this workbook not only eases your financial worries but also empowers you to share that peace with others.

So, welcome to Speak Money — where we embark on a journey of financial literacy together! You've already taken the first step by picking up this book, and for that, I commend you. To set you on your path, here are some practical tips:

Change takes time: Remember that change doesn't happen overnight in our daily financial decisions. As you absorb the wealth of knowledge in this book, give yourself the grace to break old habits gradually. Start with one or two positive financial behaviors and build from there. Don't overwhelm yourself by trying to change everything at once—crawl before you walk.

Embrace a growth mindset: Shift your perspective from fixed thinking to a growth mindset. Believe that your abilities can improve with consistent effort. Challenges and failures are part of the journey. Learn from them and keep growing.

Don't let the math intimidate you: Financial literacy revolves around math. Don't be afraid of it.

Utilize online resources, calculators, and websites to help you with financial calculations. Math is the language of financial competence.

Seek support: Don't tackle this journey alone. It's okay to feel overwhelmed or uncertain about your financial decisions. Enlist the support of a friend or mentor to go through this book with you. Seek advice from those who have walked the path before you.

Remember, you are not alone on this journey. Financial literacy is a powerful tool that can empower you to shape your financial future, and it's more enjoyable and sustainable when shared with others.

With blessings and best wishes,

Naiomi Israel

INTRODUCTION

*S*peak Money: The Cheat Code to Financial Literacy is an integral part of our educational series developed by Fulphil, the 501(c)3 nonprofit organization I founded that is committed to democratizing access to social entrepreneurial education. My journey began with a vision to empower everyone to create a positive impact in their communities and the world. While rooted in social entrepreneurship, the broader mission of our team's curriculum is to inspire students to recognize their potential for positive change and equip them with the tools to become successful, mission-driven problem solvers.

Our vision was initially sparked by a survey of over 680 high school students who attended Fulphil workshops. It revealed a significant socioeconomic disparity in access to entrepreneurship resources. This fueled our mission to provide equitable access to impactful entrepreneurship education.

We are transforming our curriculum into this published book with the hope that the content of *Speak Money* will extend beyond our classrooms. It has become a mission to democratize financial literacy on a broader scale. We aim to empower individuals of all backgrounds in homes, communities, and workplaces across the country. Since 2018, our team has worked tirelessly to democratize essential curriculum, creating and launching our financial literacy curriculum, now known as *Speak Money*. We embarked on this journey during the peak of the Black Lives Matter movement and the COVID-19 pandemic, aiming to bridge the financial literacy gap, inclusively. We envisioned a resource that would empower individuals, regardless of their background or prior financial knowledge, to take control of their financial future.

The development of *Speak Money* was a collaborative effort, guided by educators, financial experts, curriculum designers, and our own students who shared our passion for financial education. Together, we crafted a curriculum that demystifies seemingly abstract financial concepts, making them accessible to all. Our goal for *Speak Money* and for all of our other courses is to create content that resonates with everyone, breaking down barriers based on race, gender, or background.

Financial literacy should be accessible to all, regardless of their starting point. Our curriculum seeks to demystify complexity and offer guidance through the intricacies of personal finance. We believe financial literacy should be a fundamental right, not a privilege. *Speak Money* is designed to empower you to navigate the world of finance, challenge the status quo, and speak money with an inclusive voice that resonates far and wide.

In the vast landscape of financial literacy, your journey will with understanding the following chapters and fundamental concepts:

- **Chapter 1:** Imagine building your financial fortress, starting with three crucial pillars: Emergency Fund, Credit, and ROI

(Return on Investment). These pillars lay the groundwork for a stable financial future, where you can weather storms, leverage your resources, and make your money work for you.

- **Chapter 2:** In Chapter 2, we delve into the realm of Social Capital, where networks and relationships hold immense value. You'll explore retirement planning, employee benefits, disability insurance, The Family and Medical Leave Act (FMLA), and the art of negotiation. Building strong connections and understanding the systems that support your financial well-being are paramount.

- **Chapter 3:** Here, we explore the art of budgeting with various approaches, from the traditional "Pay-Yourself-First" method to the innovative "Zero-Based Budget". You'll master concepts like Income, Expenses, and Inflation, enabling you to take control of your financial destiny.

- **Chapter 4:** In this chapter, we dive into personal financial statements, dissecting cash inflows, cash outflows, and net worth. You'll learn to differentiate between assets and liabilities, unlocking the secrets of your financial health.

- **Chapter 5:** In this chapter, we will unravel the historical context, from generational wealth to the racial wealth gap. We explore the legacy of the abolition movement, sharecropping, Jim Crow Laws, and the impact of government policies on wealth distribution. By understanding these historical roots, we pave the way for building intergenerational wealth.

- **Chapter 6:** We will equip you with essential tools for navigating the financial landscape. You'll explore the world of savings, cash equivalents, and debt. We'll guide you through methods like the Snowball Method and Debt Avalanche, helping you conquer debt and establish a solid savings foundation.

- **Chapter 7:** Meanwhile, the concept of retirement may seem distant, but it's never too early to plan. In Chapter 7, we embark on the journey of retirement planning, considering future expenses, life expectancy, and various retirement accounts like Roth 401(k)s, IRAs, and annuities. You'll understand the power of compounding and the importance of employer benefits.

- **Chapter 8:** This chapter is your gateway to the world of investing. We demystify terms like diversification, stocks, bonds, mutual funds, and the S&P 500. You'll learn the strategies and principles that guide successful investors in their pursuit of financial growth.

- **Chapter 9:** Here, we will explore the world of insurance, from health coverage to life insurance and auto protection. You'll gain insights into premiums, deductibles, and the key differences between various insurance types.

- **Chapter 10:** We will delve into the intricacies of taxes, exploring topics like tax returns, IRS, tax deductions, and tax cuts. You'll gain knowledge of tax forms and concepts like tax deferral and tax-deductible expenses.

- **Chapter 11:** Here, we will uncover the world of credit, credit scores, and credit reports. You'll learn the impact of credit on your financial life and discover how to manage it responsibly. We explore concepts like compound interest, credit utilization, and identity theft protection.

- **Chapter 12:** This chapter introduces you to the world of banks, from basic accounts to wealth management services. We discuss the importance of financial institutions and the options available to safeguard your money.

- **Chapter 13:** In this chapter, we will venture into the future, exploring concepts like Web 3.0, decentralization, DeFi (Decentralized Finance), and blockchain. You'll unlock the potential of these innovations in shaping the financial landscape of tomorrow.

- **Chapter 14:** This chapter will delve into the world of digital currencies, from Bitcoin to Ethereum, exploring the fundamentals of blockchain technology and the concept of decentralized finance.

- **Chapter 15:** In our final chapter, we embark on a journey into the future, embracing concepts like tokenization, NFTs (Non-Fungible Tokens), and the Metaverse. As we navigate this new digital era, you'll discover strategies for building and preserving wealth in an ever-evolving financial landscape. With this comprehensive guide, you'll navigate the intricate web of financial literacy, empowering yourself to make informed decisions and secure your financial future in an ever-changing world.

Chapter 1
The Basics of Financial Literacy

As of January 2022, the #moneytok tag generated over 10.6 billion views on TikTok, more than #tacotuesday, #gossip #cookingtiktok, and so much more! Videos offering financial advice were going viral.[1] In just a year later, this number grew over 78%. This was huge — not only because financial advice has been becoming more accessible, trendy, and fun, but also because the conversation of the US racial wealth gap is something that is more actively being brought to public light.

However, TikTok is not the only place you need to turn to for financial advice! We've got you covered — but don't worry, we will also provide some TikTok videos to keep things fresh!

I. Defining Financial Literacy: What is it & What does it look like?

According to Investopedia, financial literacy is the knowledge necessary to make important financial decisions.[2] It can help with

---

1   The Economist Newspaper, "Personal finance is a hit on TikTok," 2022.

2   Fernando, J., "Financial literacy: What it is, and why it is so important," 2023.

decisions about budgets, debt, savings, and investing — all of which we will be covering in this course!

As mentioned, the concept of financial literacy and personal finance have been trending on a popular cultural level, but what does it actually look like? What does it even mean to be financially literate and be in a good state with your budgets, debt, savings, and investing?

The current state

You would be shocked to know that over 1 out of every 4 US households indicated they have no retirement savings, and fewer than 4 out of 10 are actually on-track.[3] Over 60% of individuals are confident in their own financial decisions.

Millennials are currently the largest share of the workforce, but they have demonstrated a low financial literacy rate, and are unprepared for a severe financial crisis, which we are going through now.[4,5] Here are the stats:

- 19% answered questions about financial concept correctly
- 43% report using expensive alternative financial services
- 50%+ lack an emergency fund
- 37% are financially fragile (meaning, they are unable to come up with $2,000 within a month in the case of an emergency)
- 44% have too much debt, specifically student debt

---

3   USAFacts, "Half of American households have no retirement savings," 2023.

4   NEFE, "Millennials show alarming gap between financial confidence and knowledge," 2017.

5   Yahoo! " New report finds only 16% of millennials qualify as "financially literate" 2020.

Further, these trends seem to be continuing. As 84% of Generation Z (AKA Gen Z) depends on their family for guidance on managing money, it becomes essential for parents to provide accurate and helpful advice.[6]

One of the main challenges behind these gaps lies in the fact that teaching financial literacy isn't as straightforward as teaching subjects like math or history…but that is why you're here, reading Speak Money!

Where you need to be

We are here to help you be in a better place financially! When we think of people with good financial standing, it is safe to think of some of the following examples:

- **Having at least 3 to 6 months' worth of cash available for an emergency fund.**[7] As we all know, unexpected challenges arise! We can never know when unfortunate events happen, so we must always think ahead and be prepared on a financial level when they happen. Life doesn't prepare you for medical emergencies, your car breaking down, or someone breaking into your home. But you can prepare yourself financially. The amount you save will vary from person-to-person, depending on your lifestyle, monthly expenses, and income.

---

6   Perna, M. C. "Why Financial Literacy isn't gen Z's sweet spot-yet," 2022

7   Saving for an emergency. How Much Should You Be Saving for an Emergency? | Wells Fargo. (n.d.). https://www.wellsfargo.com/financial-education/basic-finances/manage-money/cashflow-savings/emergencies/

- **Having good retirement savings.** We don't want to work forever, right?! At least most of us don't. There are ways to save up from the benefits you receive from your job, and/or investing a portion of your pay every month.

- **Having good credit.** You probably hear about this often. But what is credit?! Credit is the ability to borrow money or access goods or services with the understanding that you'll pay later.[8] How someone can build this ability is demonstrating their financial competence and responsibility over time. We will go into this some more later in our course.

- **Having knowledge of how your political choices impact your finances.** We know, the thought of politics will either excite or bore some of you. It is important, nonetheless. How some politicians go about passing some laws will impact taxes on your income, how much you make, and ultimately, your lifestyle. It is important to read up on the law and news.

II. So, why is financial literacy important?

Financial literacy is important for various reasons, including some of the following:

1. **Financial literacy is critical for creating social mobility and generational wealth.**

---

8   Person. (2022, July 7). What is credit & how does it work?. Capital One. https://www.capitalone.com/learn-grow/money-management/what-is-credit/

This is the first and foremost reason why financial literacy is so important. However, the fact that TikTok was blowing up with so many videos on personal finance and financial literacy caused a big conversation on why it is not something that is taught in schools as exhaustively as we would like it to be.

It's not taught in schools?!

According to Robert Kiyosaki, the author of the book, Rich Dad, Poor Dad, financial literacy is often intentionally not taught in our traditional education systems for the reasons of "helping the rich stay rich" and maintaining the wealth gap.[9] As Kiyosaki concisely puts it:

"Money is one form of power. But what is more powerful is financial education. Money comes and goes, but if you have the education about how money works, you gain power over it and can begin building wealth. The reason positive thinking alone does not work is because most people went to school and never learned how money works, so they spend their lives working for money."

In an article, he further cited a study that found only "13% of Americans were taught about investing in school. The same people surveyed believe overwhelmingly that financial literacy should be taught in school (87%), and that it should start as early as Middle School (72%)."[10]

---

9   Kiyosaki, R. T. (2023). Rich Dad, poor dad. FBV.

10   Team, R. D. P. F. (2011, September 20). A different financial education (in 17 definitive lessons). Rich Dad | Financial Education & Coaching for Everyone. https://www.richdad.com/17-financial-education-lessons

An understanding of money and how it works is imperative for social mobility and creating generational wealth, but in its own way, the US has weaponized education, which is particularly more harmful to individuals of lower socioeconomic status (SES) and people of color.[11]

2. **It is easy to let money manage your life, but you need to manage your money.**

You may have heard the phrase "live to work or work to live." Lack of financial literacy can put individuals in a vicious cycle, stuck in the "work to live" category. Often, this is part of the concept that Kiyosaki describes as how the rich make their money work for them.

What this means is, people with fewer financial resources often study to obtain a good education, so they have better chances at getting better quality jobs to help them earn more money. These individuals avoid taking risks out of fear of not being able to pay their debts, getting fired, or not having enough money needed to survive. Kiyosaki argues that, on the other hand, rich people take risks by buying and building assets that generate income in their sleep! This is the biggest takeaway of *Rich Dad, Poor Dad*.

It is important to know how to invest and what to invest in, and to always continuing to learn, to grow yourself as an asset. We will do a deep dive on this in a later unit. But it is important to note that, when we invest in things that have potential to grow, we will have

---

11   Mollenkamp, D. T. (2023, July 1). The racial gap in financial literacy. Investopedia. https://www.investopedia.com/the-racial-gap-in-financial-literacy-5119258

good ROIs. This also includes investing in yourself and growing your knowledge to help you gain unique skill sets to grow your own value.

3.   Financial responsibility is increasing for consumers.

Consumers are taking on more financial responsibility. For instance, before there was such a thing as Cash App, Apple Pay, Venmo, PayPal, and the overall existence of credit cards, people used cash for daily purchases. Today, we use credit cards more frequently.

In 2019, credit use accounted for 27% of payments, up from 24% in 2017. According to Investopedia, how we shop has also changed.[12] Online shopping is now preferred over brick-and-mortar retail shops, which also makes it a lot easier to overextend credit. Especially when you have companies like Amazon and their patented "one-click shopping," this becomes all too easy to spend and accumulate debt quickly.[13]

4.   Saving and investment options are becoming more complex.

We as consumers are now often asked to choose from various investment and savings products. These products are more sophisticated than they were in the past, which is exciting, but it almost creates the "Netflix paralysis" problem of having so many options to choose from that it becomes overwhelming!

Having more sophisticated options requires consumers to select from different options that offer varying interest rates and maturities,

---

12   Segal, T. (2022, July 5). How covid-19 changed consumer shopping behavior. Investopedia. https://www.investopedia.com/how-we-shop-now-5184434

13   Why Amazon's "1-click" ordering was a game changer. Knowledge at Wharton. (2014, September 14).

decisions they are often not adequately educated to make. These choices can impact a consumer's ability to buy a home, finance an education, or save for retirement, adding to the decision-making pressure. This can be helpful or harmful, depending on how much you decide to learn about these factors. Also, given the advancements of modern health, we now also have longer lifespans and require more money for retirement than earlier generations did. With this, the number of institutions that offer products and services to those going into retirement can also be overwhelming, further creating confusion for the consumer.

5.   If you want a good lifestyle later on, you need to start now.

When we talk about financial literacy, we have to bring up the concept of retirement. That may sound strange and even morbid because it seems so far away and you are probably already struggling to make short-term decisions, ranging from how you will save up for that car you want to if you have enough money for dinner!

However, you must start thinking about retirement now, because if you want a good lifestyle later on, you have to start building your resources up as soon as possible to get there. Everyone has their own idea of their ideal lifestyle, and it is up to you to define that. Based on what that looks like for you, you will need to figure out how to get there, based on your career choices and how you save, and build your wealth.

6.   You don't want to wait until it's too late.

Why is it so urgent to build financial literacy? We get it, it is easy to procrastinate and push things off. But it's important to start now because you want to protect yourself from debt and bankruptcy. If you've played Monopoly before, you know bankruptcy is literally GAME OVER! It is important to invest in your assets and build wealth now, which first begins with financial literacy. You don't win the game without buying homes and hotels, after all!

But games aside, it's important to acknowledge the real-life necessity of an emergency fund. Throughout our lives, we're likely to encounter unexpected financial hardships. Historical events such as the market volatility following the 2008 recession and the inflation period after the COVID-19 pandemic serve as stark reminders of this reality.

III. Your Relationship with Money

What is your relationship status…with money? Building financial literacy begins with understanding your relationship to money because it impacts your outcomes and trajectories.

We all have a different relationship with money
Everyone has a different relationship with money from how we earn, spend, and manage it. The ways our families and those around us speak about and value money influence how we process and perceive money, as well. With this, our relationships with money are constantly changing and evolving based on our own circumstances and close networks. Even individuals raised in the same household

might have different relationships with money. According to Wespath, our relationships with money lie on a spectrum of insecurity — on one end is being frugal, and on the other end is being irresponsible.[14]

We can think about our relationship with money in terms of three different dimensions: acquisition, spending, and management.

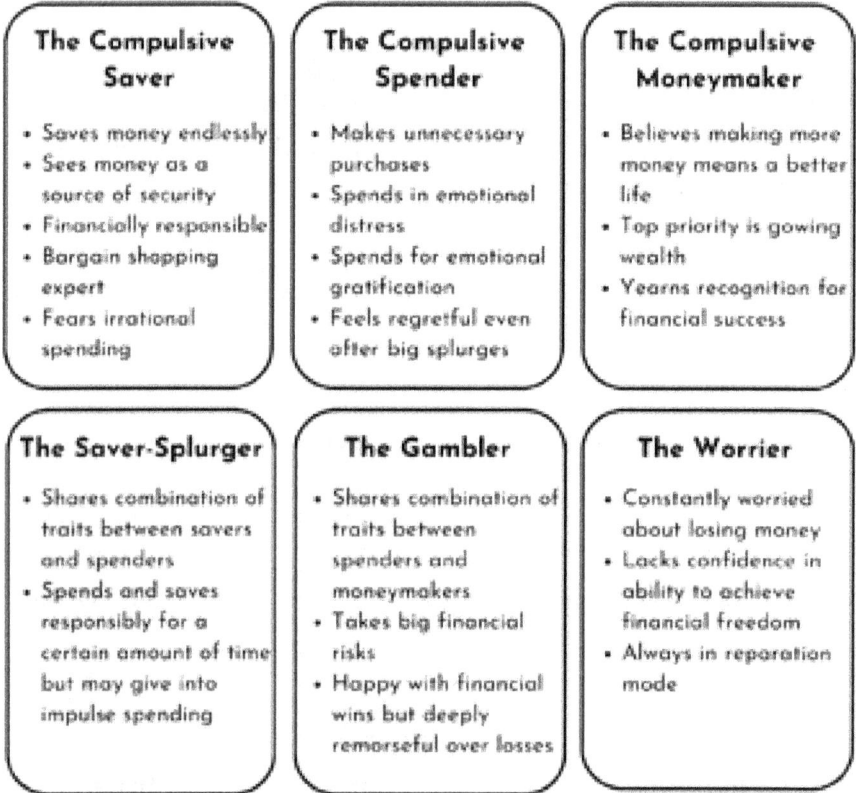

The Compulsive Saver	The Compulsive Spender	The Compulsive Moneymaker
• Saves money endlessly • Sees money as a source of security • Financially responsible • Bargain shopping expert • Fears irrational spending	• Makes unnecessary purchases • Spends in emotional distress • Spends for emotional gratification • Feels regretful even after big splurges	• Believes making more money means a better life • Top priority is gowing wealth • Yearns recognition for financial success

The Saver-Splurger	The Gambler	The Worrier
• Shares combination of traits between savers and spenders • Spends and saves responsibly for a certain amount of time but may give into impulse spending	• Shares combination of traits between spenders and moneymakers • Takes big financial risks • Happy with financial wins but deeply remorseful over losses	• Constantly worried about losing money • Lacks confidence in ability to achieve financial freedom • Always in reparation mode

Which do you identify as?[15]

---

14   Understand your relationship with money. Wespath Benefits | Investments. (n.d.). https://www.wespath.org/health-well-being/health-well-being-resources/financial-well-being/understand-your-relationship-with-money

15   Honda, K. (2020). Happy money: The Japanese art of making peace with your money. John Murray Learning.

Regardless of your personality type and your relationship with money, ask yourself: What influenced you to have the relationship with that you do? Think of those around you and certain experiences that have been influential in defining how you decide to spend, earn, save, and invest money.

We nonetheless all have a different relationship with money, and understanding our relationship is the first step to success. Once you are able to properly identify your relationship, you can define what financial success means to you. This is going to be different for everyone. Some might imagine financial success as an extravagant lifestyle, while others may imagine something simpler but filled with value in other ways. There is no right or wrong answer. It is fully dependent on your preferences and what you like that you believe makes you happy.

What does financial success look like to you?

IV. Cheat Code Recap

1. Financial literacy is the knowledge necessary to make important financial decisions.
2. Financial literacy is important for creating social mobility and generational wealth.
3. The sooner you begin building financial literacy and putting it to action, the better.
4. Everyone has a different relationship with money and a different definition for their financial success.

Chapter 2
Careers

N ow that we have created a foundation of your understanding of the basics of financial literacy, your own relationship with your personal finances, and what financial success looks like to you, it is time for us to help you figure out how to achieve those goals! We are going to teach you through reverse-engineering and back-tracking, first through mapping out your potential career paths that can help you achieve the lifestyle you want for yourself. Let's begin!

I. Mapping Out Your Potential Career Paths

Understanding what your goals are: Lifestyle & Work Personality

When you are young, people often ask you what you want to be when you grow up. Maybe they will ask you to draw a picture of what that looks like—a firefighter, a chef, a police officer, a doctor, etc. However, what people really should be asking is how you want to be, and more specifically, what type of life you want to create for yourself. What we want to be can determine the lifestyle we want to live, but it may not be exactly what we want holistically. We want you to think one step deeper. Afterall, you may not know what you want to do, but you may know what you want your future lifestyle to look like.

What type of life do you want to create for yourself? What does your everyday look like from start to finish? What would you do to have fun? How much would you want to work? What annual salary do you need to achieve that life? Your answer to this question is the first step needed to help you define success for your future. How does this make you feel about the lifestyle you envision for your future self?

Our goal here is not to create a 10-year-plan, but rather, to begin thinking about how you can leverage your attributes to help you get there.

Afterall, the thing is, no matter how much you plan for your life, things will not always go as planned — which is also important to embrace. But to be able to have a sense of direction to rely on as a North Star is something that can always be reassuring and also something to look forward to.

What is one thing you can do now as a next step to help you make some headway towards the lifestyle and career you imagine for yourself?

How to get your foot in the door + build social capital

Financial literacy and mapping out your goals and financial success are all just part of the first step. However, it is not only about financial capital. You must also know how to build social capital.

Social capital refers to the potential that individuals have in being able to secure benefits and invent solutions to problems through membership in social networks.[16] This is where the concept of "it's not what you know, it's who you know" comes into play.

Similar to financial literacy and financial capital, social capital cannot be built overnight. It takes time. Oftentimes, to be able to achieve our goals, we need social capital.

When building social capital, it is important to remember that it is not about getting our foot in the door, but rather to make sure that we are already inside the door before it opens again for the right opportunity. For instance, if you are applying for a job that you believe will help you reach your financial goals and dream-lifestyle, you will have a much better shot at getting a job offer if you already know the person who is interviewing you, or if you already know someone who puts in a good word for you at the company you are looking to work for.

It is much easier said than done, and, it is unfortunate to say, but this is why the "side door" concept of the Rick Singer college admissions scandal was so effective.[17] But we want to leverage it for good! While the scandal was a very ugly look into the power of social capital, it is nonetheless a testament to the efficacy of social capital to helping you get the opportunities you are looking for.

But how does one even begin to build social capital, especially if you don't have any existing networks?

One of the first steps is to let others know you are trying to build your networks. It is okay to be open about it! If anything, it can also

---

16   Kenton, W. (2022, November 27). What is social capital? definition, types, and examples. Investopedia.

17   Admission through the 'side door' - the chronicle of higher education. (n.d.). https://www.chronicle.com/package/admission-through-the-side-door/

let others feel like they are already being helpful just by meeting and getting to know you! Let others around you know that you are trying to meet more individuals who have aligned goals or can be interesting to chat with as you figure out your next steps.

To be able to get others to feel like they are in a position to help you is invaluable on a personal and psychological level. Here are some helpful tips you should keep in mind as you are building your network of peers and mentors:

1. **Have a clear vision and goal in mind.** Before you search or reach out, you should have a well-defined reason for why and how it will help you. It will be much easier to find someone who is willing to help if they know exactly what you need help with! The more specific you are with what you are looking for, the more willing others will be to guide you!

2. **Conducting research on your industry.** Who are the leaders in the industry you are most interested in? Is there anyone local to your area that you could meet with? Can you find anyone on LinkedIn that you could coffee chat with?

3. **Use your existing network.** Say you have an idea of what you want to do in mind. Don't be afraid to ask the people you already know to connect you with someone else! Do your parents have any friends that could help? What about your teachers? What about your friends' parents? What about your friends? What about that one summer camp you attended or the clubs you joined in high school? Or even the people who come to speak at your school assemblies? Have faith in the six degrees of

separation (the theory that all people are six or fewer social connections away from each other)![18]

4. **Reach out!** Once you have a list of potential people you can contact, it's important to establish a line of communication that works best for both of you. Not everyone will be willing or have the time to help, which is why you want to have several contact points to work with. One way that works well is through email! Be sure to introduce yourself, what you want to do, and what type of guidance you are looking for. You don't have to ask, "Will you be my mentor?" Instead, ask for their advice on a certain project or topic you would like more insight on. This could be a great way to open conversation!

For example, here is the first message that Naiomi (our foreword writer) wrote to our me.

"Hi Tiffany! I'm Naiomi and I just want to say your work through Fulphil really inspires me! As someone also interested in social impact, specifically economic stability, I am wowed by your heart to teach students not just to dream, but supply them with practical tools and resources to "fulphil" them. I'm really interested in starting a nonprofit and would love to get some wisdom about the technicalities, and also just talk more about your work. We could continue messaging here or even set up a short Zoom call if you are comfortable. Let me know what works ☺ Thanks for your time!"

---

18   The science behind Six Degrees. Harvard Business Review. (2014, August 1). https://hbr.org/2003/02/the-science-behind-six-degrees

Naiomi's Template & Tips:

- Always make sure to acknowledge what you admire about the person and their work.
- Connect that admiration to yourself and your personal goals.
- Create some small ask for further communication, like a 15-minute call.
- It's always easier to reach out to people who are connected to you in some way. Did you go to the same high school or college? Grow up in the same town? Work at the same job at different times? Use that as a launching off point, if applicable!

5. **Keep in touch!** Once you have established your line of communication, be sure to set up a call or some type of meeting, and continue to set up those calls and meetings, if the person seems serious about helping you! Depending on what you are looking for from this mentorship relationship, you can continue to reach out and establish a monthly meeting time if it deems fit.

   You are probably wondering, but WHAT on earth do I even keep in touch about? Sometimes, you may want to stay in touch, but you feel like you have nothing new going on for you personally, or you feel like you are taking too much and offering nothing to the relationship.

   One cool idea is to keep up to date on the news of your shared field or interests. For example, if you are meeting with an entrepreneur you look up to, you might want to talk about a new startup or business model you learned about and ask for the other person's opinion. Or if you share a common interest in cooking, you might want to share a recipe that you loved or tried! The possibilities are endless!

II. Careers with Benefits

Oftentimes, we think so much about the job that we don't think enough about the benefits that come with it.

What are employee benefits?

Employee benefits include various types of non-wage compensation provided to employees in addition to their normal wages or salaries.

The four main types of benefits are:

- **Medical/health insurance.** Medical or health insurance is often one of the top benefits that organizations offer. However, health benefits can vary based on the size of the organization, the industry it is in, and your time and contribution. Some organizations will only cover basic costs, while others might also include dental care and eye care. It is important for you to find out about what kind of doctors' appointments are covered under your company and learn whether your employee covers everything, or if you will need to pay a portion of it.

- **Life insurance.** Life insurance, which covers funeral expenses and other costs, is also a benefit that employers offer. Sometimes this can be automatic when you start working at a new company, and other times you will have to sign up to receive this benefit; speak with your HR department for details. You can also find out how much of a premium your employer covers and if you can purchase additional coverage.

- **Retirement plans.** Retirement plans can greatly differ, but a common benefit for for-profit companies is a 401(k) since many companies no longer offer pension plans. Nonprofits offer a 403(b) plan more often. When analyzing the retirement plan that your company offers, find out what percentage of your salary you can set aside and what your investment options are. Also, many employers will match employee contributions up to a certain amount. Employer matching percentage can increase the longer you stay at the company (if offered). It is highly recommended to max out how much your company matches to maximize retirement balance.

- **Disability insurance.** Disability insurance is also an important benefit that many companies offer. This is different from worker's compensation insurance, which covers accidents that may happen while working. Disability insurance covers accidents, illnesses, or injuries that happen off the clock that prevent an employee from working.[19] Keep in mind that disability insurance coverage will cover a percentage of an employee's salary, so make sure you are aware of the percentage that the company provides to you. Additionally, find out if your company provides both short-term and long-term disability insurance and how long each of those terms lasts.

---

19   Kagan, J. (2022, March 14). Disability income (DI) insurance: What it is and how it works. Investopedia.

Other types of employee benefits include:

- **FMLA.** The Family and Medical Leave Act requires employers to allow employees to take leaves for medical and family reasons.[20] Examples include pregnancy leaves — employees can take up to 12 weeks after the birth of the child in the United States.

- **Tuition Reimbursement or Remission.** Employers may fully or partially reimburse employees for education, as long as the courses or major of study is related to your current role. After reimbursement, employers will require you to stay with the company for a period of time, or you will have to pay them back per policy.

- **Paid Time Off/Vacation Days.** Most corporate employers will have paid time off or vacation days. It is best to see how much is offered when hired — usually three weeks at first, and this will accrue with the time you are staying at the company. Sometimes, vacation days are negotiable, should your offered salary not meet your expectation.

- **Learning and Organizational Development.** Most companies do offer courses to enhance your skills and abilities to help you better succeed in your role or move up the ladder of promotion. Examples would include leadership development and public speaking. Feel free to consult with your HR department to see if anything is offered. The courses are usually free of cost.

---

20   Family and medical leave (FMLA). DOL. (n.d.).

It is great that a lot of companies offer insurance — and if they don't, fight for it! However, do you have to take the insurance? You can always opt out, depending on your own needs and priorities, to align with your own lifestyle. Sometimes, you can negotiate to opt out of insurance to receive a higher salary.

III. Negotiation

Whether it is your company benefits or the flea market, you should negotiate. Negotiation is the process of facilitating discussion to come to an agreement. Negotiation is all about compromise. The goal of negotiation is to make sure that both sides feel content about the outcome and find a way to meet in the middle. A successful negotiation is when both sides feel like they still "won."

The #1 rule is to ALWAYS negotiate.

When it comes to reviewing job offers and the employee benefits that come with them, you ALWAYS negotiate! It may seem scary, especially the first time. However, companies expect you to negotiate. If you are being offered a salary that feels too low, propose what you want or what feels right, within reason. Or perhaps you are happy with the terms. If you are content with the offer, you should still negotiate — don't be afraid to bump it up a bit or ask for additional benefits!

Some asks you can make when negotiating your salary or benefits:

- Increase your salary by $X

» Salary transparency is becoming more popular! You can utilize resources like LinkedIn to get a salary range for your position, and then negotiate from there based on your experience/expertise.

- Opt out for a specific insurance type if you don't need it, and negotiate for a higher salary (if a company is not paying for you insurance, they should have some extra dollars available)

- If you are moving to a new city, ask about receiving relocation costs.

- Ask if you can get a bonus. Or if you have a bonus already, ask if you can increase it.

- Ask them to define your PTO (paid time off). Some companies nowadays offer unlimited PTO. That doesn't mean you get to work a week and chill the rest of the year, though! Have them specify what exactly it means. Sometimes, there is a lot of pressure when you are working at companies like these because it is up to you to determine when you feel good enough with your work to ask for time off.

  » Absolutely do the research to understand employee experiences. This perk may sound perfect, but when the time comes for you to take that day off, your supervisor may respond differently. So definitely make sure you are well-informed, and that you and your potential employer are fully on the same page.

You might have lots of reasons behind why you are asking for more. However, it is always a good rule of thumb to keep it concise.

Do not say more than you need to. You don't always need to feel obliged to explain yourself.

It is terrifying at first, we know! But once you can successfully negotiate, you will feel empowered to negotiate in every context moving forward. The worst case is that you get a "no." A "no" is not a defeat; rather, it's an integral part of the learning process, providing insights for future discussions. A "no" is perhaps the default outcome — but negotiating positions you one step closer from turning that "no" into a "yes". With every experience, you'll gain confidence and a better understanding of how to navigate and advocate for your interests. Remember, every successful negotiator has faced their share of rejections, and it's through these experiences that they've honed their abilities. Keep in mind, your worth is not defined by a single response, but by your willingness to grow and persevere.

More than half the battle is the preparation.
Always be prepared with all your key points in your negotiations. Before any of your negotiations, be sure to come prepared with the following:

- Identify reasons for why your proposal may also be beneficial to the other side.
- Identify reasons for why the other side's proposal may also be beneficial to you.
- Know what you want to get out of it. What does success look like?
- What are your own motivations and interests?
- What are the motivations and interests of the other side?

- Identify fallback options and compromises you would feel comfortable with.

- Identify fallback options and compromises you believe the other side would feel comfortable with.

- Identify any potential weaknesses in your position.

- Identify any potential weaknesses in the other side's position.

It is important to consider the motivations and interests of both sides prior to going into a negotiation. Make sure you do the homework!

IV. Cheat Code Recap

1. Social capital refers to the potential that individuals have in being able to secure benefits and invent solutions to problems through membership in social networks.

2. When building social capital, it is not about getting our foot in the door, but rather to make sure that we are already inside the door before it opens again for the right opportunity.

3. Employee benefits include various types of non-wage compensation provided to employees in addition to their normal wages or salaries.

4. The #1 rule is to ALWAYS negotiate.

Chapter 3
Budgeting

I. What is budgeting? Why is it important?

Budgeting is the process of creating a plan to spend your money. The spending plan is called a **budget**. Creating this spending plan allows you to determine in advance whether you will have enough money to do the things you need or would like to do. Budgeting can allow you to create short- and long-term financial goals, whether it's saving up for that cool product you saw on TikTok, concert tickets, a vacation trip, starting a business, college tuition, your first home, or retirement.

More reasons for why budgeting is important include:

1. **Help you identify bad spending habits.** We have all had those scary moments of nervously opening our bank accounts or wallets, waiting to see how much money we have left after splurging or hanging with friends. Our minds racing with the fear that we have truly gone broke, but still holding onto a faint sliver of hope that maybe we didn't spend as much as we thought... It is so important for us all to keep track of finances and know how much we spend and understand our overall spending patterns. By doing so, we can learn where we might

be spending too much and figure out ways we can cut down and spend our money more wisely. We want to open our accounts and wallets with pride (not anxiety!).

2. **Strategize how to live within your means to work towards your savings goals.** Yes, it might hurt when you realize you can't afford that Nintendo Switch you've been eyeing…yet. But with the help of a budget, you will know how much it will actually take for you to be able to buy it. It will also help with your long-term goals, as well, to figure out how many years it will take for you to pay off your student loans or how much money you will need before you go into the retirement you want.

3. **Land your "dream retirement".** Carefully planning your finances will allow you to enjoy your later years with peace of mind and security. It involves estimating the costs of your desired lifestyle, which may include travel, hobbies, or even a second career, and then working backwards to save the necessary funds. By budgeting wisely now, you can set aside enough to not only cover basic expenses but also fulfill dreams you've saved for your golden years. This proactive approach allows you to retire on your terms, with the freedom to choose how you spend your time, whether that's with family, in leisure, or pursuing passions that you've waited to explore.

4. **Control your credit.** Did you know that the average credit card debt per household reached $5,525 in 2021? It is hard to know if you overuse and abuse credit cards until you are drowning

in debt.[21] When we only had cash, it was much easier to know whether or not you were living within your means. Keeping a budget makes us more conscious of our spending habits, so we are not mindlessly spending and swiping!

5. **Be prepared for emergencies.** Like we said, unexpected challenges arise! Things always spring up out of nowhere in life, whether it's fixing a flat tire, replacing your broken phone or laptop, repairing a broken faucet, or paying for medical bills. When it happens, you don't want to feel unprepared or realize too late that you don't have enough money to afford what you need to do. Budgeting will help you allocate small amounts of money over time to go into your emergency fund.

6. **Money is one of the biggest stressors in the world.** A budget helps create financial stability. Sadly, only 47% of Americans use budgeting methods to keep close track of their spending, according to the National Foundation for Credit Counseling in 2020.[22] By tracking expenses and following a plan, a budget makes it easier to pay bills on time, build an emergency fund, and save for major expenses such as a car or home. Overall, a budget puts a person on stronger financial footing for both the day-to-day and the long term. To be able to have confident control of your budget will help you relieve that stress and help you obtain the lifestyle you want.

---

21   Wendel, S. (2021, September 7). State of credit 2021: Rise in scores despite pandemic challenges. Experian Insights.

22   5 simple budgeting methods. LendingTree. (2023, September 22)

II. What goes in a budget?

INCOME
Monthly income

- Job
- Student loans/grants/scholarships
- Gifts
- Side hustles

As you earn income, it is important to remember to aim to consistently build identity capital by investing in yourself. **Identity capital** comprises the repertoire of skills and experiences that pave the way for greater professional opportunities.[23] While certain positions may seem to offer limited growth, every job can contribute to your resume in valuable ways. For example, roles in retail, such as a barista or cashier, can develop customer service expertise, leadership, and operational knowledge, all of which are essential skills for those aspiring to advance to management roles or transition into corporate positions within the industry. By investing in your development, you acquire knowledge and abilities that enhance your potential to live the life you envision and increase your future earning power.

---

23   Lee, I. (2020, November 25). Defining and building identity capital for takingthe best steps in your life. Goalcast.

EXPENSES

Debts

- Student loans
- Credit cards
- Personal loans
- Taxes (federal, state)

Leveraging credit cards wisely can be a strategic component of managing your finances. Financial experts often recommend using credit cards for routine purchases to benefit from rewards such as cash back and points, particularly with cards offering bonuses for specific categories like groceries and fuel. The key is to treat credit cards as a payment method rather than additional income and to spend only what you can fully pay off at the end of each billing cycle. This approach allows you to enjoy the perks of credit cards without accruing debt. Additionally, when you have surplus funds, consider using them to pay more than the minimum due on your balances, targeting the principal and interest, to expedite debt reduction and strengthen your financial footing.

Education/School

- Tuition
- Books, supplies, etc.
- Trips

If you're in college, you likely only receive loans, grants, and scholarships once per semester. You may only use these funds to pay your school expenses once per semester, but it's a good idea to average that cost out per month, so you have an idea of the impact of those expenses on your monthly budget. If you need more income, check with your financial aid office to see if you qualify for Federal Work Study or look into a part-time job on or off campus.

Entertainment and Gifts

- Events, going out, subscriptions (concerts, movies, magazines, apps, hobbies, books, music, games)
- Cable/satellite services
- Online streaming, gaming services
- Gifts
- Charitable donations

We all need some room to let go once in a while. Whether that's going out to dinner, a night out on the town, or ensuring you can catch your favorite shows, you should keep an eye on this category. While difficult, this can be a good category to cut back on if you need a little extra somewhere else.

Everyday Consumables

- Groceries
- Clothing
- Pet care (food, grooming, etc)

You might find that considering some simple changes to your eating habits could positively impact your budget. Maybe try experimenting with cooking at home more often, which can be a delightful way to save money and discover new favorite dishes. Carrying snacks could gently curb the urge to swing by a café or a fast-food restaurant. And if you enjoy eating out occasionally, why not keep an eye out for coupons or special deals? They can add a sprinkle of savings to your dining experiences without sacrificing the pleasure of a meal out. These small, voluntary shifts in your daily routine can subtly transform your spending habits and contribute to your financial well-being.

Healthcare

- Insurance (premiums, copays, deductibles, etc.)
- Medications
- Gym memberships

Navigating healthcare expenses requires an understanding of certain key terms that impact your budget. Premiums are the regular payments you make to have health insurance, whether monthly, quarterly, or annually. Copays are fixed amounts you pay for covered services, like a doctor's visit or prescription drugs, and deductibles are the amounts you pay out of pocket before your insurance starts to cover costs.

Familiarizing yourself with these terms can help you anticipate and plan for medical expenses more accurately. After considering these fundamental costs, remember that incorporating preventative health measures — such as a nutritious diet, regular exercise, and good dental hygiene — can contribute to overall well-being and potentially reduce the need for costly healthcare services. Annual check-ups are also vital, as they can detect health issues early on, which is not only beneficial for your health but can also be more cost-effective in the long run.

Transportation

- Vehicle (loan, fuel/gas, maintenance, insurance, parking, licensing)
- Public transportation, Ride sharing
- Bicycle (maintenance, licensing, etc.)

Transportation can be a significant expense, but there are smart ways to manage it within your budget. For instance, swapping a car for a more economical vehicle, like a scooter, could substantially lower your costs. Consider also the benefits of biking to work; it's not only cost-effective but also great for your health and the environment. Additionally, take the time to compare insurance rates periodically. Shopping around for insurance can uncover better deals, ensuring you're not overpaying for the coverage you need. These changes can lead to sustainable savings and a lighter financial footprint.

Housing

- Dorm fees, rent, mortgage, insurance
- Utilities (electric, sewer/water, gas, garbage)

- Phone
- Internet

If you think you're spending too much here, consider finding a cheaper place or getting a place with a roommate. Utilities and communications are generally easy areas to cut back on, if needed. Call your utility companies to ask about ways to save, consider more eco-friendly light bulbs, and unplug all electronics when you're not using them.

Travel

- Airfare
- Hotels/Airbnb/Overnight stays
- Food
- Transportation
- Entertainment

When considering travel expenses, it's important to remember that travel isn't solely for leisure—often, it's necessary for personal reasons such as family commitments, events, or even self-care. If you're finding that travel costs are adding up, take a moment to reflect on the purpose of each trip. For leisure trips, a balanced approach might be to plan one or two meaningful vacations rather than several shorter getaways, focusing on quality over quantity. For personal travel, assess if every trip is essential and if there are more economical options available, such as off-peak travel times or alternative transportation methods. As a rule of thumb, aim to allocate a portion of your income that aligns with your financial goals and necessities, leaving room for these important personal journeys.

Unexpected expenses

- Savings/Emergency fund
- Medical costs (personal, veterinary)
- Vehicle (repairs, travel, etc.)
- Replacing lost or broken items

It's always a good idea to have an emergency fund for unexpected expenses. If possible, try to put away some money each month for this category; you'll be happy you did if something goes wrong! It's also a category you can put more or cut back, depending on where your finances are throughout the year. Think of your savings as your first payment you make each month to yourself; you're investing in ensuring your future is secure.

III. How to create a budget/budgeting system

Different methods of budgeting

A possible precursor to a budget is monitoring your spending habits for a couple weeks to a month. You don't have to change any spending habits yet; use this time to figure out what money is going where and how often. That way you can actually see the types of things that you splurge on a little too much, and you will become aware of the actual cost of things before you go into making your budget.

There is no "right" way to budget, as it depends on your own goals and personal work ethic. Here are a few of the most commonly practiced budgeting techniques:

1. **Zero-based budget.** This is the idea that income (how much you make) minus all actual, possible, unexpected, future, and for-fun expenses (how much you spend) equals zero. This method is best for individuals who have a set income every month, as it requires you to know your expenses as accurately as possible. Not even a penny is unaccounted for! In this budget, you have a set amount to allocate to all of the categories we listed above, equaling your income; this way you don't get tempted to make spontaneous purchases.

2. **Pay-yourself-first budget.** This is the concept where, every time you get paid, you first set aside a specific amount for personal savings and debt repayment goals before paying off any other expenses.

3. **Envelope system budget.** This is similar to zero-based budgeting, but it is all in cash. You will put together different envelopes for each type of monthly expense. For instance, one envelope will have your monthly expenses for groceries, while another will contain money for transportation. This creates control on a more physical level since it deals with cash, but is not recommended for people who prefer credit cards or don't feel comfortable having cash on hand.

However, it is important to be cautious of inflation on the rise in today's economy when it comes to the envelope system budget. Just so we are all on the same page, inflation is an economic term for when there is a general increase of prices and a decrease in the value of money. Over a period of time, the value of your savings can be reduced due to inflation, and it is a much bigger difference when it comes to cash.

4. **50/30/20 budgeting.** This is a budgeting system where you set aside 50% for necessary expenses, 30% for discretionary expenses, and 20% for savings and debt payments or investing.[24] This is helpful if you are ball-parking your expenses and aren't keeping track of every single cent, since you don't need to get stuck on the proportions.

5. **The "No" budget.** This might be self-explanatory. In this system, you are listing out items you will absolutely restrict yourself from spending money on. Instead of creating a budget, you can:

   • Keep track of your overall account balance.
   • Know when recurring bills hit your account.
   • Set aside money for savings and extra debt payments.
   • Spend whatever is leftover without overdrawing on your account.

   This is usually an easier method if you already have discipline in your own spending habits.

---

24   Whiteside, E. (n.d.). The 50/30/20 budget rule explained with examples. Investopedia.

One of the most important things you must keep in mind when budgeting is to check your budget often. It is easy to set up, but always important to check back in, reevaluate it, and update your expenses accordingly, month-over-month, to ensure you are staying on track.

Also, it is important to always be honest with yourself. If you are not honest on the things you are spending money on, you are only lying to yourself (and your bank account!). And, be open to your wants/needs changing and your budget style changing with them. It is not going to be easy, but it is important to set goals and be disciplined.

IV. Cheat Code Recap

1. Budgeting is the process of creating a plan to spend your money.
2. Budgeting is important to help you identify bad spending habits; strategize how to live within your means to work towards your savings goals; control your credit; be prepared for emergencies; and, ultimately, help you relieve your stress and obtain the lifestyle you want.
3. The main components of a budget are your income and expenses.
4. Different budgeting strategies include the zero-based budget, the pay-yourself-first budget, the envelope budget, the 50/30/20 budget, and the "no" budget.

Chapter 4
Creating Financial Statements & Understanding Wealth

Personal **financial statements** are methods to help you plan your budget and also set goals for increasing your net worth. The two main types of personal financial statements are:

- Personal Cash Flow Statement
- Personal Balance Sheet

I. Personal Cash Flow Statement

Cash is king.

Ever heard of the phrase, "Cash is king"? It refers to when companies or individuals have large amounts of cash on-hand and/or liquid assets (meaning easy to turn into cash), allowing them more flexibility in their spending for their business operations or personal lives. The phrase can take on a variety of meanings, but it ultimately means that cash is superior to other forms of payment.

To really understand how to build financial stability and go beyond to achieve your financial goals, it is important for us to fully grasp the concepts of cash inflow and outflow.

Cash inflow[25] is the cash that you are gaining. This is a term that can be used to describe the cash that a business is bringing in, as well as the cash that you are earning as an individual. Cash inflows often include:

- Salaries
- Interest from savings accounts
- Dividends and capital gains from investments
  - » **Dividends** are a distribution of profits by a company/corporation to its shareholders.[26]
  - » **Capital gains** are the overall increase (gains) from a capital's overall value determined once it is sold.[27]

On the other hand, **cash outflow** is the opposite — it is the cash that is spent or goes "out." Types of cash outflows include:

- Rent or mortgage payments
- Utility bills
- Groceries
- Gas
- Entertainment (books, movie/concert tickets, streaming subscriptions, eating out, etc.)

---

25   Medleva, V. (n.d.). What is cash inflow: Definition and meaning. What is Cash Inflow: Definition and Meaning

26   Hayes, A. (n.d.). Dividends: Definition in stocks and how payments work. Investopedia.

27   Chen, J. (n.d.). Capital gains: Definition, rules, taxes, and asset types. Investopedia.

The term, **cash flow**, or **net cash flow**, is used to describe the difference between your cash inflows and cash outflows.[28]

$$Net\ Cash\ Flow = Cash\ Inflow - Cash\ Outflow$$

The better case is having positive net cash flow, which means you have more than you spent. Negative cash flow means that you spent more than you earned, which either puts you in debt or bankruptcy.

We measure our cash flow through the use of a **personal cash flow statement**. A personal cash flow statement is a type of financial statement that measures your cash inflows and outflows for a specified period of time (monthly, annually, etc.).[29]

Creating your personal cash flow statement

Feel free to use this template provided (make a copy of it) or access another template of choice from our premade templates! To access our templates, you can go to our website to build your monthly budget and annual budget at **www.fulphil.org/class-projects.**

Why understanding cash flow is important + How to increase your cash flow

Understanding our cash flow is important because it can help us figure out our main sources of income and how we can spend our money. We are here to help you learn some ways you can improve

---

28   Hayes, A. (n.d.-a). Cash flow: What it is, how it works, and how to analyze it. Investopedia.

29   Hayes, A. (n.d.-a). Cash flow statement: How to read and understand it. Investopedia.

your cash flow so you can reach your financial goals. Some strategies include the following:

- **Increase your income.** Find ways to get a raise or get the job you want to be able to pay you what you need to have enough buffer room to live the life you want. Also, many people find it helpful to have multiple streams of income through freelancing their talents/skills, working side hustles, investments, and other means of making extra income.

- **Cut down on your expenses.** Figure out what your spending patterns are. Perhaps you spend more money than you would like to on clothes. You don't have to go gold-turkey and resist the temptation to buy clothes completely; instead, think of how you can cut down your clothes expenses by 10%?

- **Pay off or refinance your debt.** Debt is something that always makes cash flow fairly risky because it must be repaid. Refinancing is simply a fancy word that means you are replacing the terms of your debt under new terms and interest rates.[30]

II. Personal Balance Sheet

Meanwhile, a **personal balance sheet** is the second type of personal financial statement, which provides an overall snapshot of your **wealth**, or your **net worth**, (the sum of your **assets** and **liabilities**) at a specific period in time.

---

30   Kenton, W. (n.d.). Lifestyle inflation: What it is, how it works, example. Investopedia.

Net worth = Assets - Liabilities

Assets

Assets are essentially anything you own. There are various types of assets. We will create four separate categories of them here.

- Liquid assets: This is whatever can be turned into cash fairly easily and without losing value. Some examples include:
  - » Checking accounts
  - » Money market accounts
  - » Saving accounts
  - » Cash
- Large assets: These usually consist of personal items. Usually, in a balance sheet, large assets must reference their market value or the price of similar assets.
  - » Homes
  - » Cars
  - » Boats
  - » Artwork
  - » Furniture
- Digital assets: This is anything that can be stored digitally and be uniquely identified.
  - » NFTs
  - » Cryptocurrency

- » Documents
- » Audio/Video files
- » Logos
- » Websites
- » Copyright
- Investments
  - » Stocks
  - » Bonds
  - » CDs
  - » Mutual funds
  - » Real estate
  - » Cryptocurrency
- Fixed assets: This is any type of asset that can have a useful life of more than a year. In this case, a useful life refers to the approximate amount of time that the asset can help you earn money. Fixed assets are more often used in a business setting, as opposed to a personal one.
  - » Intangible assets: These are assets that lack a physical presence and cannot be touched.
    - Goodwill (not the store! We mean actual goodwill, which is the overall value to a company or things that cannot really be quantified)
    - Brand equity
    - Intellectual property (trade secrets, patents, and copyrights)

- Licensing
- Customer lists
- Research and Development (R&D)

» Tangible assets: These are assets that have a physical presence

- Cash
- Real estate
- Land
- Jewelry
- Wine/Alcohol
- Furniture
- Real estate
- Inventory/Equipment/Machinery

We will define the different examples of these categories in later sections, so don't worry if it sounds like a mouthful for now. There are various ways to define assets, which you may have noticed from some overlapping examples across categories. There is no need to get nitty-gritty with this; the goal is (1) to understand the concept of an asset and (2) to understand that there are various ways to define different types of assets that can make up your wealth.

Liabilities

Liabilities are what you owe. This could include your outstanding payments, bills you still owe on an asset if you had an initial down payment (the amount of money that you pay in purchasing an expensive product or service if you don't pay the full amount up-front), credit card debt, and other loans.

Creating your personal balance sheet

Feel free to use the template provided (make a copy of it) or access another template of choice from our premade templates! To access our templates, you can go to our website to build your personal balance sheet at **www.fulphil.org/class-projects**

Why is understanding net worth important?

Now that we understand the concepts of assets and liabilities, it is important to understand why net worth is important to prioritize.

Your net worth shows whether or not you are in good financial standing. Your net worth is an indicator of your overall wealth — not just how much you make but also how much you own (your assets) and how much you owe (your liabilities). In the long game, having good control over your net worth is most important for financial planning, like buying a home or business, or figuring out your plan to reach your retirement goals.

Rich vs. Wealthy

As we mentioned, your net worth is a good indicator of your wealth; however, it is not a good indicator of your riches. Let's break down what this means.

A rich person has money but might not have a good handle on their money. A rich person has good cash flow, which means that they have a high paying job and a good income. But oftentimes, when people have higher income, they can afford more for their lifestyle.

Consequently, their spending is often higher. This is not always the case, but it is fairly common. It is a phenomenon called **lifestyle inflation**. Lifestyle inflation is when your monthly expenses increase as you earn more. For example, someone who is already living above their means (meaning they spend more than they make) is likely to increase the level of spending as their income increases.[31]

Lifestyle inflation can be a problem because it is hard to build wealth in the long term. Did you know that lottery winners are actually more likely to go bankrupt in three to five years than the average American?! If you have lots of money coming in but also lots of money going out (lots of cash inflow and lots of cash outflow), it can become challenging to keep up with it.

In summary, this means that rich people are not always wealthy.

A wealthy person has good assets. This means they own a lot beyond their income. This can mean different things for different people, depending on the types of assets they own and how they try to grow their assets. With this, wealthy people have a higher chance at keeping their wealth (especially for future generations, #GenerationalWealth) than rich people do, due to: (1) the ability to grow their assets and (2) the consequences of lifestyle inflation.

In summary, rich people let their money control them, wealthy people control their money. And not all rich people are wealthy, but all wealthy people are rich.

_____

31   Changes in US.family finances from 2016 to 2019 - federal reserve board. (n.d.-b).

III. Cheat Code Recap

1. Personal financial statements are methods to help you plan your budget and set goals for increasing your net worth.

2. The two main types of personal financial statements are cash flow statements and balance sheets.

3. Net Cash Flow = Cash Inflow - Cash Outflow

4. Net worth = Assets - Liabilities

5. Being wealthy is not the same as being rich. Wealthy people have a higher chance at keeping their wealth than rich people do due to (1) the ability to grow their assets and (2) the consequences of lifestyle inflation.

Chapter 5
Disparity & Building Wealth

I. Average American Net Worth + Generational Wealth

According to the Federal Reserve Board, they issue a Survey of Consumer Finances every three years to learn more about household income and net worth.[32] As of September 2020, American households had an average net worth of $748,800.

As Nerd Wallet points out, this is a fairly high number.[33] It is because the average net worth is driven by higher socioeconomic status individuals with higher earnings and generational wealth (any kind of asset that families pass down to their children or grandchildren, whether in the form of cash, investment funds, stocks and bonds, properties, or even entire companies).

The average net worth for American households is driven up due to the following reasons:

---

32   The average net worth by age: How does yours compare?. NerdWallet. (n.d.)

33   Hoffower, H. (2020, October 12). Millennials dominate the US workforce, but they're still 10 times poorer than Boomers. Business Insider.

The Generational Wealth Gap

The **generational wealth gap** is the difference between the amount of wealth accumulated within one generation relative to the wealth accumulated within another generation. Business Insider wrote that Boomers (individuals born between 1946 and 1964) are 10x wealthier than millennials (individuals born between 1981 and 1996), in addition to Gen Z.[34] The generational wealth gap exists because of the following reasons:

- Most of Gen Z has not entered the workforce yet. As of 2022, the oldest Gen Z is aged 24 and under, which means most have not entered the workforce yet, so we can't expect them to earn income or much wealth.

- Boomers are moving into retirement while the majority of millennials are beginning to transition from entry-level to mid-career positions in the workforce.

- Many older millennials were hit hard by the **Great Recession.** The Great Recession was a severe global economic downturn that began with the 2008 financial crisis, deeply impacted many older millennials. This generation found themselves embarking on their post-college careers or furthering their education when the crisis unfolded, marked by massive job losses, investment declines, and the bursting of the housing bubble. The ensuing **affordable housing** crisis resulted from this economic turmoil, which contributed to a scarcity of reasonably priced homes. This situation left many millennials financially strained, struggling

---

34   Hoffower, H. (2020a, October 12). Millennials dominate the US workforce, but they're still 10 times poorer than Boomers. Business Insider.

to manage student loan repayments and facing rising living costs that surpassed expectations.

- Younger millennials had been establishing and progressing from their entry-level careers right when the COVID-19 pandemic hit.[35] This caused many people across the country to deal with layoffs, pay cuts, and furloughs. Because younger millennials are the least established at the companies they work for, they are the most likely to be let go in times of economic instability.

- All millennials are having to wait longer for the transfer of wealth from their parents, who were also hit by the Great Recession.

In effect of these economic and social factors, some outcomes include:[36]

- One year of college tuition increased from $10,000 thousand for boomers to $25,000 for millennials.

- 5% more boomers owned a home than millennials at the same age. The cost of a home has also increased by over $122,000 between the two generations.

- 3% more boomers owned stocks compared to millennials at age 40.

---

35   Hoffower, H. (2020a, May 8). Younger workers are hit hardest in the coronavirus job market, and it spells bad news for millennials and gen Z. Business Insider.

36   Hicks, P. (2022, February 2). Generational wealth gap: Millennial vs boomer wealth gap. Trust & Will.

Based on these factors, millennials are more behind on building their wealth compared to any other generation that preceded them. According to NPR, millennials are 40% behind previous generations in terms of building their wealth.[37] Millennials only hold 4.6% of wealth in the US, while boomers hold 53.2%.[38] Boomers are ten times wealthier than millennials and two times wealthier than Gen X (individuals born between 1965 and 1985).

II. The Racial Wealth Gap

The racial wealth gap is the disparity in assets of typical households across race and ethnicity. To understand how serious this problem is, the Federal Reserve Bank found that white families with an unemployed head of household had almost double the wealth of Black families with a fully employed head of household.[39]

In this section, we will be focusing mostly on the Black-White racial wealth gap. And we might already know that slavery obviously hindered the prosperity of Black Americans in this country, but, boy, has policy failed Blacks economically continuously after that:

---

37   Rosalsky, G. (2021, April 27). There is growing segregation in millennial wealth. NPR.

38   Tanzi, A. (2021, October 5). Gen X sees wealth jump 50% in pandemic. Bloomberg.com.

39   Hamilton, D., & Darity, W. A. (n.d.). The Political Economy of Education, Financial Literacy, and the Racial Wealth Gap.

A History of Economic Injustice

Slavery:

During slavery, Black people were dehumanized and seen as property, something that added to the wealth of whites, meaning Blacks had zero net worth. Black people in this nation were used as literal investment property, adding wealth to their enslavers' pockets for their free labor — all while enslaved people were denied all rights, including decent living conditions, education, and income.

Failed Reconstruction:

Reconstruction refers to the period after the Civil War, between 1865 -1870, where US Administrators tried to reconstruct society as a place for Black people to be free and equal citizens.[40]

The "Good"

First, Blacks were promised 40 acres and a mule to relocate from their former enslavers.[41, 42] Then, policies like the 13th, 14th, and 15th Amendments along with the Civil Rights Act of 1866 gave Blacks the opportunity to be citizens, use public accommodations, gain land from previous enslavers, vote and hold political offices, get employed, and have autonomy to open their own businesses, schools, and colleges.

---

40   A&E Television Networks. (2023, April 24). Reconstruction - Civil War End, changes & act of 1867. History.com.

41   Brown, D. L. (2021, April 15). 40 acres and a mule: How the first reparations for slavery ended in betrayal. The Washington Post.

42   Reconstructing citizenship. National Museum of African American History and Culture. (2022, August 22).

Actually, historically Black colleges and universities (HBCUs) Morehouse and Howard, were both opened during this time![43] Also, the Freedman's Savings Bank was created to help Black citizens reach financial independence, where over 60,000 Black people deposited over $1 million dollars![44]

Nevertheless, as you can probably guess, the situation was not peaches and rainbows, and white political leaders did everything in their power to hold white people up economically, socially, academically, and legally.

The Bad

In our US History classes, we are often taught about the North and the South and their contrasting views on slavery; however, let's not forget that the entirety of America (even the North) was still very much racist by today's standards. Despite the North's efforts in furthering the abolition movement, which sought to promote freedom from slavery, they still did not treat Black people equally — hence the infamous phrase "separate but equal".

First, and thought to be the most harmful economically, whites were pardoned and given back the land that tens of thousands of Black people were living on because of the 40 acres given to them. Sharecropping, in most cases, became a fancy word for slavery. The Freedman Savings Bank's all-white trustees lost most of the savings

---

43   Historically Black Colleges and universities - the development of hbcus, academic and social experiences at hbcus, conclusion. StateUniversity.com. (n.d.).

44   Chatman, A. (n.d.). Black Americans' rocky relationship with banks can be traced back to an institution that promised wealth but collapsed after just 9 years. Business Insider.

that were deposited, leaving black depositors with little to no savings. Groups "protecting" whiteness, like the KKK, began violently terrorizing and spreading harmful messages about Black people being lazy and criminal. Then, policies known as "Black Codes" legalized racism. Just to give a few examples, these laws:[45]

- Legally prevented Black people from borrowing money to buy and rent land.
- Punished employers who offered Black workers higher wages.
- Established racial segregation in public places.
- Outlawed Blacks from speaking in court, making it illegal for a Black person to testify against a white person

Not to mention that if you were Black and somehow managed to be successful economically, you were often killed, your assets stolen and/or your property or business destroyed.

Jim Crow laws expanding the wealth gap

Jim Crow Laws were a set of laws that ultimately promoted the following:[46, 47, 48]

---

45   The Black Codes and Jim Crow laws. Education. (n.d.).

46   What was Jim Crow. Jim Crow Museum. (n.d.).

47   Lee, T. (2019, August 14). How America's vast racial wealth gap grew: By plunder. The New York Times.

48   Jim Crow laws and racial segregation. Social Welfare History Project. (2023, September 12).

Exclusion from wealth building programs

Blacks were excluded from government-funded wealth building programs like President Franklin Roosevelt's New Deal. This project helped build a solid middle class through social programs like social security and minimum wage while America was going through the Great Depression. However, most Black people were not granted the same protections, as jobs available to them were primarily in the domestic and agricultural fields, and thus did not qualify.

Redlining

When the Fair Housing Act was passed in 1934, it allowed white working- and middle-class families to purchase homes through making much cheaper monthly payments with interest. However, the Fair Housing Administration (FHA) refused to insure mortgages in and near Black neighborhoods, a phenomenon known as redlining. The FHA also subsidized (giving free financial assistance) for builders to mass produce homes, as long as none of the homes were sold to African Americans. Literal proximity to Blackness was said to make a home 'hazardously' risky to insure and lower the value of a home.

Even today, upward mobility (the ability for someone to rise to a higher position economically and/or socially) is lowest in areas with the most segregation, and highest in places with the most diversity.

The FHA, the Home Owners Loan Corp (an organization that provided government loans after the stock market crash that sparked the Great Depression in 1929), and the Veterans Administration, designed a map to indicate the safest places to insure mortgages. If

Blacks lived in or near an area, that area was colored red to indicate high risk.

Their exact reasoning for an area to be uninsurable could have been "a growing infiltration of negroes," which was accompanied by zero evidence that Blacks would have defaulted (not paid) on loan payments.[49, 50]

Blacks were instead given substandard housing, barely (if any) assistance, and often paid more for public housing in terrible conditions than whites had to pay in mortgages. By the time redlining was abolished, the value of the homes whites were granted for a fraction of the cost were now four times the value, and Blacks could not afford to relocate.

Where you live, even today, can determine what kind of education you get, how much law enforcement is paid (law enforcement actually get paid more to work in more affluent areas!), and the relationship between officers and citizens, health conditions, and wealth/ upward mobility.

Redlining is not just about discriminating against Blacks, but white people being supported and boosted even when they faced financial difficulty.

Employment

Before Title VII of the Civil Rights Act, white people held the power to fully discriminate on the basis of race. Not only were whites allowed to not employ you, but they also had free range on how low

---

49   Mapping inequality: Redlining in new deal america. Bunk. (n.d.).

50   How redlining's racist effects lasted for decades. Bunk. (n.d.-a).

they could pay you, leaving Blacks with significantly less pay than their white coworkers for the same job.[51, 52]

Education

The segregation of schools meant Black schools had far fewer resources.[53] In the South, the NAACP found that Georgia's per pupil spending for white students was almost eight times more than per pupil spending for Black students. In the 60s, Martin Luther King Jr. wrote about the disparities in the Northern states:

"Statistical evidence revealed in 1964 that Chicago spent an average of $366 a year per pupil in predominantly white schools and from $450 to $900 a year per pupil for suburban white neighborhoods, but the Negro neighborhoods received only $266 per year per pupil."

Poor People's Campaign

Did you know Martin Luther King Jr. was starting a new movement before he was assassinated? They might have left this detail out of your history books, but Martin Luther King Jr. was leading a new civil rights movement, along with the Southern Christian Leadership Conference (SCLC), focused on economic equality called the **Poor People's Campaign.**[54]

---

51   The Civil Rights Act of 1964: A long struggle for freedom the segregation era (1900–1939). Library of Congress.

52   Title VII and employees' legal rights. Justia. (2023, October 15).

53   The Achievement Gap in Education: Racial segregation versus segregation by poverty. Brookings.

54   Poor People's campaign. Poor People's Campaign. (n.d.).

King and the SCLC had been effective in getting the Civil Rights Act of 1964 passed, then the Voting Rights Act of 1964, but their next goal was to create the largest and most sustainable effort of civil disobedience in American history! King believed that African Americans and other minorities would never reach complete citizenship until they were economically secure. Their goal was to address the various issues of housing shortages for poor people, unemployment, and the overall impact of poverty on millions of Americans, primarily people of color. From May 14th to June 24th, 1968, protestors including poor African, Hispanic, Native Americans, and white Americans, would have daily demonstrations of civil disobedience, starting with a huge march in Washington DC.[55]

They demanded a $12 billion Economic Bill of Rights that would guarantee employment for people able to work, income for people unable to work, and an end to rampant housing discrimination.

The March was supposed to happen May 14th, but Martin Luther King was assassinated April 8th, just one month earlier.[56] Though his advisor and new SCLC president, Ralph Abernathy took over and led the movement, King's death and the Vietnam War greatly overshadowed their efforts, and the government barely scratched the demands they were asking for.

---

55   A&E Television Networks. (n.d.). Civil Rights Movement: Timeline, Key Events & Leaders. History.com.

56   March on Washington for Jobs and Freedom. The Martin Luther King, Jr. Research and Education Institute. (n.d.).

Stats on Today's Racial Wealth Gap

The racial wealth gap is just as bad as it was in the 60s. This is because since that time, while white wealth skyrocketed, Black wealth has virtually remained stagnant.

An article in The Washington Post cites the following statistics:[57]

- Income disparities among racial groups evolve differently over generations, with Hispanic and Asian Americans nearing parity with white Americans while Black Americans and American Indians lag behind. In nearly all US neighborhoods, Black boys ultimately earn less than their white counterparts from families with similar incomes. In 1968, the typical middle-class black household possessed $6,674 in wealth, while the median white household held $70,786.

- By 2016, the wealth gap had widened, with middle-class black households having $13,024 in wealth compared to $149,703 for the median white household.

- The proportion of millionaire families differs significantly by race, with one in seven white families achieving this status compared to just one in 50 black families.

- As of 2016, it took the combined net worth of 11.5 black households to match the net worth of an average white US household.

---

57   WP Company. (2020, June 5). Analysis | the black-white economic divide is as wide as it was in 1968. The Washington Post.

White wealth surges; black wealth stagnates

Median household wealth, adjusted for inflation

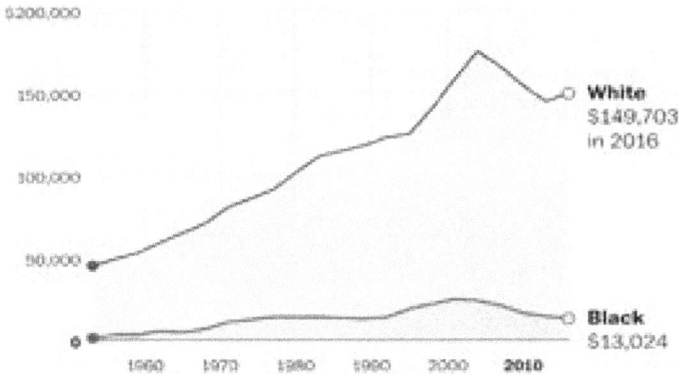

Image cited from Washington Post.

Further, according to Opportunity Insights—a non-profit organization headed by Harvard economics researcher and professor Raj Chetty—has the mission of identifying obstacles that restrict upward mobility and finding solutions that empower people to rise up from poverty and reach better life outcomes (AKA the American Dream). Their work has shed a lot of light on the opportunity gaps in this country that keep poor people poor. Two notable highlights include the following:[58, 59, 60]

58   Racial disparities. Opportunity Insights. (2018, November 7).

59   Demographic trends and economic well-being. (2016, June 27). Pew Research Center's Social & Demographic Trends Project.

60   The opportunity atlas. The Opportunity Atlas. (n.d.).

- Income disparities among racial groups evolve differently over generations, with Hispanic and Asian Americans nearing parity with white Americans while Black Americans and American Indians lag behind.

- In 99% of all US neighborhoods, Black boys ultimately earn less than their white counterparts from families with similar incomes.

Children's Incomes vs. Parents' Incomes, by Race and Ethnicity

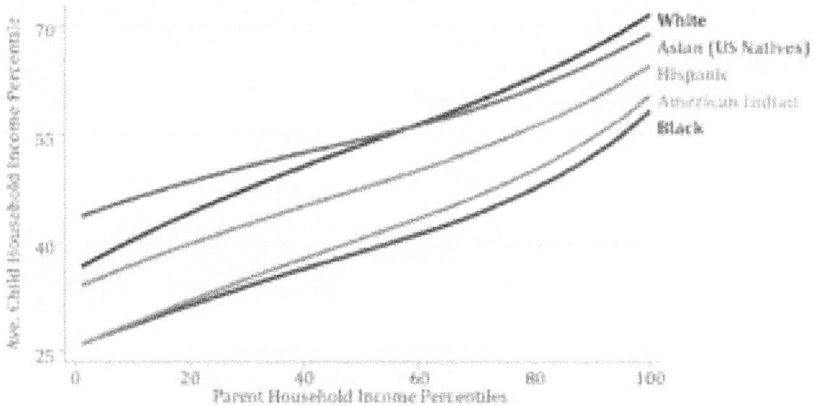

Image cited from Opportunity Atlas.

Opportunity Insights has uncovered that the Black-white racial wealth gap is improving the least, and the racial wealth gap is actually caused primarily by the gap between Black men and white men.[61] There are many theories as to why this is; however, it is crucial to emphasize that their research has shown that inequalities in family

---

61   Badger, E., Miller, C. C., Pearce, A., & Quealy, K. (2018, March 19). Extensive data shows punishing reach of racism for black boys. The New York Times.

factors like the rates of parental marriage, educational attainment, and wealth, along with variations in individual capabilities, have only a small impact on the generational divide between Black and white individuals.

Stats on Today's Intergenerational Wealth Gap

Intergenerational wealth refers to assets that the older generation in a family passes down to the younger generation. This is thought to be one of the greatest predictors of wealth.[62]

Further, based on the findings of Opportunity Insights, The New York Times published a popular article citing the following:

1. Income gaps between race: Imagine, John, a white man, earns significantly more than Marcus, a Black man, even though both have similar job positions and qualifications.

2. No gender income gap for Black vs. white women: Imagine, Emily, a white woman, and Keisha, a Black woman, earn similar salaries as marketing executives in the same company.

3. Intergenerational income gap for boys: Imagine, Jamal, a black boy, raised by two parents with a combined income of $140,000, is projected to earn about as much as Liam, a white boy raised by a single mother with an income of $60,000, despite the vast difference in their family backgrounds.

4. Limited non-white children in the top income percentile: Imagine, Maria, a Latina child, is among the very few non-

---

62   DesRoches, D. (2019, May 16). Georgetown study: Wealth, not ability, the biggest predictor of future success. Connecticut Public.

white American children who start their lives with family income levels in the top percentile, providing her with unique opportunities compared to her peers.

The racial wealth gap is highly complex, with numerous contributing factors. Historical laws hindered Black progress while favoring white financial prosperity. Despite overwhelming evidence of the impact of discriminatory laws on African Americans' wealth-building abilities, myths falsely place blame on Black individuals.

Myths about the Racial Wealth Gap

In What We Get Wrong About Closing the Racial Wealth Gap, published by Duke University's The Samuel Dubois Cook Center on Social Equity, we learn about the 10 biggest myths of solutions to the racial wealth gap problem.[63]

These myths propose commendable strategies for individual wealth accumulation. However, the issue lies in their misapplication as solutions to the racial wealth gap. While they may indeed benefit disadvantaged minorities, their implementation alone would not suffice to eliminate the persistent racial wealth disparity.

The 10 myths include the following within the categories of improved education, homeownership, and wealth building:

---

63   What we get wrong about closing the racial wealth gap - Duke university. (n.d.-c).

Better education and harder work will close the racial wealth gap

- Myth: Education and Wealth: Usually, when a Black family is led by someone who went to college, they have less money than a white family led by someone who didn't finish high school. This might seem surprising, but it's what the data shows.

- Myth: Jobs and Money: When families have jobs, they tend to have more money than those without jobs, no matter if they're Black or white. But even when Black families have jobs, white families without jobs still have more than ten times the money. And even when white families don't have jobs, they often have more money than Black families where the head of the household works full-time.

Homeownership

- Myth: Low Wealth Without Homes: When families don't own a home, both white and Black families usually don't have much money. But Black families who don't own a home have very little money, like only $120, which isn't enough to cover a week's worth of expenses.

- Myth: Difference in Wealth: The information also shows that white families who don't own homes have 31 times more money than Black families who don't own homes. This means that it's not just about owning a home that makes you wealthy; it's often about having money in your family from the beginning. And having money makes it easier to buy homes, especially expensive ones where you end up owning a lot of the home.

- Myth: Spending Habits: On average, Black people tend to be more careful with their money than white people. They found that when Black and white people make the same amount of money, white people tend to spend 1.3 times more than Black people.

Wealth Building

- Myth: Diverse Asset Portfolio: Having different kinds of valuable things like houses, stocks, or businesses doesn't explain why white people usually have more money than Black people. However, it's actually having money in the first place that allows you to have different valuable things.

- Myth: Financial Choices: When people don't have much money, it's not because they make bad choices or don't know what to do with their money. It's because they don't have enough money to make choices. So, they end up using services that charge a lot and are not fair to them because they don't have better options.

- Myth: Financial Literacy: Knowing how to manage your money is important, but it doesn't help much if you don't have money to manage. It's like knowing the rules of a game but not having the game pieces.

Wealth builds wealth. If you already have money, it's easier to make even more money. This is because you need money to start with to invest or do things that will make more money.

So...What will *actually* close the gap?

Economists usually come to two solutions that may actually close the Black-white gap:

1. **Reparations**: Based on studies, it would take approximately $11 trillion (which is around $275,000 for each of the 40 million descendants of slavery) to bridge the gap.[64]

2. **"Baby Bonds"**: The most frequently discussed example is "Baby Bonds," where an amount ranging from $1,000 to $3,000 is placed in an investment or savings account for every Black newborn.[65] The specific amount depends on the family's existing wealth. These accounts would be overseen by the US Treasury until the account holder reaches the age of 18.

However, both of these ideas are still just theories, and some people say it's impossible to get enough support for them in politics. We've never tried something like this on a larger scale in our country before. Even though it would make a big difference right away, some experts like Raj Chetty from Opportunity Insights think that it might not work in the long run. This is because there are many things blocking Black people, especially Black men, from moving up the wealth ladder. So, this solution might only help for a short time.

But there are also many economists who believe that this plan could really close the wealth gap. What's more, they say it's important because other groups that faced unfair treatment in the past, like Japanese Americans who were put into internment camps during

---

64   Darity, W. (2021, September 24). Why reparations are needed to close the Racial Wealth Gap. The New York Times.

65   The Samuel Dubois cook center on social equity. (n.d.-c). https://www. socialequity.duke.edu/wp-content/uploads/2019/12/ICCED-Duke_BabyBonds_ December2019-Linked.pdf

World War II, were given a presidential apology and $20,000 each as compensation.[66]

Then What's the Point of This Course?!

At Fulphil, we recognize that financial literacy alone is not something that will close the racial wealth gap, but rather serve as your toolkit to navigate the world we live in. Our team believes everyone should have access to the knowledge and skillsets they need to build the life they want to live.

III. Cheat Code Recap

1. Generational wealth is any kind of asset that families pass down to their children or grandchildren, whether in the form of cash, investment funds, stocks and bonds, properties or even entire companies.

2. The generational wealth gap is the difference between the amount of wealth accumulated within one generation, relative to the wealth accumulated within another generation.

3. The racial wealth gap is the disparity in assets of typical households across race and ethnicity. It roots deep in US history and also has systemic influence with our education systems.

---

66   Qureshi, B. (2013, August 9). From wrong to right: A US apology for Japanese internment.

4. There are various myths about the racial wealth gap but some solutions that economists predict to have potential to close it include reparations and "Baby Bonds."

Chapter 6
Savings & Debt

I. Savings

W hen we increase our cash flow, we are increasing our **savings**. Savings is the total amount of money that you have remaining after you spend money from your income.[67] Savings comes in the form of cash equivalents. **Cash equivalents** are items that are similar to cash and have value, like treasury bills and notes, commercial papers, and certificates of deposit.[68] They are essentially almost any form of a bank deposit.

Types of savings

Common types of savings include the following. To make things interesting, we will relate these types of savings to examples you can find within your average game of Monopoly.

- **Emergency funds:** If you've ever played Monopoly, imagine that you have $300 Monopoly dollars used in the case you get an unlucky turn, whether it's having to pay someone off

---

67   Kagan, J. (n.d.). What are savings? how to calculate your savings rate. Investopedia.

68   Chen, J. (n.d.-b). What are cash equivalents? types, features, examples. Investopedia

for landing in their spot, "Get Out of Jail," or paying random fees that you did not expect to get. Just like how rolling dice is unpredictable, so is life and its financial burdens. Obviously, you would want to have more than $300 for an emergency fund!

- **Short-term and long-term goals:** Some common examples we have brought up include things like retirement, college tuition, buying a car, the downpayment of our first home, and so much more. In Monopoly, this would be the equivalent of turning your rent into a home, or your group of homes into a hotel!

- **No savings:** This means that you don't have any savings and you are living "paycheck to paycheck," without enough money to pay for emergency situations, and might have the risk of falling into debt or bankruptcy. If you've played Monopoly, this is the equivalent of needing to Pass Go every round if you can't make enough money from other players paying you, or running out of money if you have to pay someone for rent or not being able to pay your Monopoly fees to "Get Out Of Jail."

Types of savings accounts

There are a few different types of savings accounts that are offered by banks with different features, depending on the bank you use.[69]

- **Checking accounts:** An account that you deposit money into that does not gain interest. You do get the ability to make ATM withdrawals and get a debit card that takes directly from the money in this account. There are little to no restrictions on the

---

69   Lake, R. (2023, September 27). 6 types of savings accounts. Forbes.

amount of times you can use the funds from these accounts (unless you spend all your money of course!)

- **Savings accounts:** A savings account is an account that you can deposit money into that gains interest. There are restrictions on how often you can withdraw from these accounts.

- **Money market accounts:** A money market account usually offers a higher interest rate than a traditional savings account, and also offers checking account privileges of being able to easily withdraw money. It is essentially a mix of a savings account and a checking account.

- **Certificate of Deposit (CDs):** This is a type of account where you can deposit a larger amount of money with a higher interest rate than any non-investment account, but you can't touch your money for a specified period. The longer you decide to hold it in the account the higher the interest rate usually is.

Your Savings Rate

Calculating your savings rate

Because we all have different incomes and life situations, we all have different savings rates. Your savings rate is the percentage you have remaining/saved that is not spent from your income.[70]

Savings rate = Savings / Disposable Income

---

70   Kagan, J. (n.d.-a). What are savings? how to calculate your savings rate. Investopedia.

For example, your savings rate would be 30% if you had $300 in your savings and $1,000 in disposable income. This means that when you earned $1,000 from working however many hours at your job, you saved $300 of that $1,000.

$$30\% = \$300 / \$1,000$$

This is similar to a business' gross margin, which is the percentage of their profit divided by their total income.[71]

$$Gross\ Margin = Profit / Net\ Income$$

For instance, if you started a company that sold sustainable jewelry for $10 per bracelet and you made $4 from each bracelet sale (meaning it costs $6 to produce each bracelet), then your gross margin would be 40%.

$$40\% = \$4 / \$10$$

What is a good savings rate?

As mentioned, the 50/30/20 rule is often the rule of thumb for savings. 50% of your income goes towards your necessities, 30% goes to discretionary items, and at least 20% goes towards savings.

---

71   Bloomenthal, A. (n.d.). Gross margin: Definition, example, formula, and how to calculate. Investopedia.

It turns out that the average personal savings rate in the US as of March 2022 is 5%, according to the Federal Reserve.[72] This is sub-optimal, but everyone has different living situations. Our goal is to help make sure you can build up a good savings rate so you will not have to live paycheck-to-paycheck and not let your money control you.

II. How can I grow my savings?

Improving your cash flow

As mentioned in our previous unit, some ways you can increase your savings is by increasing your cash flow. Here are some methods you can use to do so:[73]

- **Increase your income.** Find ways to get a raise or get the job that pays you what you need to have enough buffer room to live the life you want. Also, think of side hustles or ways to make extra active or passive income!

- **Cut down on your expenses.** Figure out what your spending patterns are. Perhaps you spend more money than you would like to on clothes. You don't have to go cold-turkey and resist the temptation to buy clothes completely; instead, think of how you can cut down your clothes expenses by 10%.

- **Pay off or refinance your debt.** Debt is something that always makes cash flow fairly risky because it must be repaid. Many

---

72   Moskowitz, D. (n.d.). 10 ways to loosen up your cash flow. Investopedia.
73   Personal saving rate. FRED. (2023, September 29).

people think having debt is okay, but it is exponentially harder to become financially stable with debt, as it always means you have a negative cash flow.

Savings Accounts vs. Investing

Our savings accounts are often safe places to put our money, but they are known for having low rates of return. It is the money that we do not put at risk with investments or spending. However, when we want to grow our savings, that is when we must invest, which often has the chance of putting our money at risk. This is why we recommend investing with money that you can afford to lose. Of course, no one likes losing money, but if losing this money would mean a negative cash flow or balance sheet then *do not invest it!*

Why investing works: Time value principles/interest

In order to understand how we can grow our savings, we must first grasp the concept of the **time value of money (TVM).**[74] TVM is the concept that a dollar today is worth more than a dollar in the future if you don't do anything with it or "leave it under the mattress."

Why is this? This principle holds true because money that you make today can be wisely invested and potentially grow into becoming a much larger amount into the future. A dollar bill will have the same value, but the thing is, you can do much more with the money because you earn interest over time. If you invest it, you could maybe grow it by 10x and have $10. If you don't do anything, your dollar bill will remain a dollar bill without growing, and perhaps even be worth less

---

74   Fernando, J. (n.d.). Time value of money explained with formula and examples. Investopedia.

in value due to **inflation** — as we mentioned in a previous section, inflation is an economic term for when there is a general increase of prices and a decrease in the value of money.

This is also another reason why the phrase "cash is king" holds true — it is best to invest cash where there is an opportunity for good return, as opposed to not investing it.

III. Debt

Why we have debt + Types of debt

If you can recall our previous section that mentioned the concept of liabilities, debt is a type of liability. **Debt** is the money you owe to another individual or corporation that you borrowed from.

We have debt because when we need or want to make large purchases, we may not have all the money we neud to pay it all up-front. Some common types of debt are student loans, credit card debt, auto loans, bank overdraft charges, medical bills, overdue bills, utility bills, overdue taxes, and more.

The problem with debt is, it does not easily go away. It is not like a game of Monopoly where you can declare bankruptcy and quit the game. You will have to find a way to pay it off.

In 2019, the total average debt per American is $80,000. The top debts per individual are often the following:[75]

- Auto loan (individual average of $19,000+)
- Credit card (individual average of $5,400+)

---

75   DeMatteo, M. (2023, May 23). The average American has $90,460 in debt-here's how much debt Americans have at every age. CNBC.

- Student loan (individual average of $34,800+)
- Personal loan (individual average of $16,400+)

Over four years, all these numbers have increased by approximately 10%.

How to approach debt

Acknowledge and list out your debt. The first step to approach debt is similar to therapy — acceptance. Don't ignore your debt! This step will first begin with identifying all your debt. Here are some questions you can ask yourself:

- What account is your debt under?
- What type of debt is it?
- How much debt do you owe?
- What is the interest rate? (How much interest do you have to pay for your debt the longer you wait to pay it off?)
- How long do you have to pay it off?
- How much do you have to pay at minimum per month? And what is the maximum you can pay every month?

Next, you want to make sure you add this all into your balance sheet, which you now should know how to do!

Figure out your budget. Going back to our previous question, "What is the maximum you can pay every month?" it is important to review your budget and ask yourself how much you can personally afford to pay off at a time. You don't want to pay it all off and realize that you must live paycheck-to-paycheck. On the other hand, you also don't want to pay the minimum amount and end up paying way more over time in interest (and possibly never pay it off).

Leverage your savings. To understand the best way to pay off your debt, you will need to figure out how you can leverage your savings (e.g. improving your cash flow, investing, etc.)

Some additional debt repayment strategies include the following:[76, 77]

- **The Debt Snowball:** This is where you pay your smallest debt back as quickly as possible. You put all your focus on one debt at a time from smallest to largest, putting all your efforts into paying it off ASAP. People often like this method because it is a fast and easy quick win to build momentum into your confidence. Though this may not be the most effective math-wise, personal finance is all about habits and behaviors. The snowball method rewards behaviors faster, making it more likely for you to stay on the right course to eventually pay off all of your debt.

- **The Debt avalanche:** You're probably wondering what is up with all these snow references for debt?? Well, like snow, it can really pile up over time! Debt avalanche is a strategy where you pay the largest or highest interest rate debt as quickly as possible. People often like this because paying off a big debt can give you confidence and a sense of control over your life. It also

---

76   How to pay off debt faster. How to Pay Off Debt Faster – Wells Fargo. (n.d.).

77   Eneriz, A. (n.d.). Debt avalanche vs. Debt Snowball: What's the difference? Investopedia.

gets rid of big interest, as well. This is also the most efficient way math wise to pay off your debt! But do keep in mind because you start with your largest debt, it can take much longer to pay off.

- **Debt consolidation:** This is where you combine debts into a single account and continue to avoid any debt until after it is all paid off. This creates potential lower interest and greater focus since all the debt is in one account.

Everyone's debt repayment strategies will vary depending on their situation, so when choosing one, make sure to find what best suits your needs!

IV. Cheat Code Recap

1. Savings is the total amount of money that you have remaining after you spend money from your income.
2. Savings rate = Savings / Disposable Income
3. You can grow your savings by increasing your income, cutting down on your expenses, or paying off or refinancing your debt.
4. Debt is the money you owe to another individual or corporation that you borrowed from.

Chapter 7
Retirement Planning

I. What is retirement planning & Why is it important to think about now?

Retirement planning, according to Investopedia, is the process of leveraging financial strategies of saving, investing, and distributing money to sustain yourself during retirement once your paid work ends.[78] This is not just about how much money you have in the bank but also about your lifestyle, when you choose to retire, where you want to live, and more.

How you plan for your retirement is the ultimate test of how financially literate you are. Retirement planning combines all of the concepts we have taught you from the previous sections: assets, liabilities, income, and expenses. But now, we will add in the concepts of accounting for our **future expenses** and **life expectancy**.

Control your money, don't let *it* control *you*.

We know it might feel early for you to be thinking about retirement when you haven't even entered, or are barely entering, the workforce.

---

78   Kagan, J. (n.d.-c). What is retirement planning? steps, stages, and what to consider. Investopedia.

But retirement planning is so essential to your long-term happiness with your lifestyle, and core to teaching financial literacy!

Like we mentioned in our first section, we don't want to have to work forever!

If you want a good lifestyle later on, you have to start building your resources up now to get there. Everyone has their own idea of their ideal lifestyle, and it is up to you to define that. Based on what that looks like for you, you will need to figure out how to get there based on your career choices and how you save and build your wealth.

More importantly, it is so important to start as soon as you start your full-time job, either straight out of high school or college. Within the first week of your new job, immediately do research and enroll in what your company has to offer so that retirement contributions start as soon as your first paycheck.

By the time it happens, you can only do so much.

Retirement planning is simply not something you can procrastinate on and start the night before it's due like your school projects. It requires lots of thought and intentionality over a long period of time — if you haven't started yet, the right time to begin your retirement planning was yesterday! But as the popular Chinese proverb puts it, "The best time to plant a tree was 20 years ago. The second-best time is now."

II. How to go about retirement planning

Figure out your "magic number"

How much do you need to actually retire? This amount is going to be different for every person.

For a while, there has been a rule of thumb for needing $1 million to be able to retire and have a comfortable lifestyle. More recent professionals have used the 80% rule, which states that you need enough money to live on 80% of your income in retirement. If you had an average income of $100,000 per year, you would need savings of $80,000 per year for 20 years, which is $1.6 million. If $1.6 million is your magic number, what is your plan to get there?

As we mentioned, there are many savings plans, like the 50/30/20 rule. But if you were to do the math and save 20% of your $100,000 annual income, you would be saving $20,000 per year. But $1,600,000 divided by $20,000 is equal to 80 years! We do not want to — nor do we actually have the time — to be working 80 years until we can retire comfortably. You would likely be over 100 years old by then!

So, how do we do it?

Don't worry, you will not have to work every day for the rest of your life. We will help you work smart and figure out how to receive employee benefits from your employer and other investing methods to get there faster than 80 years.

As we mentioned in an earlier unit, employee benefits are various types of non-wage compensation that employers provide to their employees in addition to their normal wages or salaries.

Leverage your employer: 401(k) and 403(b)

401(k)s and employee matching

401(k) and 403(b) plans are now more popular for employee benefits. Roth 401(k) , also known as 401(k), plans can be offered by for-profit companies, while Roth 403(b), also known as 403(b), can be offered by non-profit organizations and the government to their employees.[79, 80]

401(k) is also known to provide more flexibility when choosing your investments.

- A 403(b) can only provide mutual funds (Remember, a mutual fund is a company that pools money from various investors and invests that money in securities, like stocks, bonds, etc.) and annuities (annuities are long-term investments issued by an insurance company to protect you from the risk of outliving what you earn from your income). This is not a bad thing, but it is just less flexible. There are still thousands of mutual funds to choose from, and annuities can also provide a good retirement income if you choose the right one.

- For 403(b), it is recommended that you do not distribute your funds until you are 59 years old, because if you do so before then, half of your funds may be subject to taxes and early withdrawal penalties. For a 401(k), you have to wait until you are 59 ½ years old to use your funds without any penalties.

- If you work for two different companies where you can get a 403(b) and a 401(k), or if your job offers both, every dollar you put in can reduce how much you can contribute to your 401(k). This is because there are annual limits (2022: $20,500) that you can add to each account individually, so if you have both, you can only contribute the max overall. For example, if in 2022 you

---

79   Retirement plans faqs regarding 403(b) tax-sheltered annuity plans. Internal Revenue Service. (n.d.).

80   Team, T. I. (n.d.). 401(k) and 403(b) plans: What's the difference? Investopedia.

contributed $10k into your 403(b), you would only be allowed to put up to $10.5k into your 401(k).

Within these plans, your employer has the option to match what you invest up to a certain amount. For instance, if you contribute three percent of your annual income to your plan account, your employer can match that (this is called **employer match**). That means that the amount you are investing from your income is doubled to be six percent! Your employer would deposit that additional three percent into your retirement account. Note: financial advisers say the employer match is one of the only times you will ever hear them say "FREE MONEY"! It is recommended that if your job offers an employer match, that you contribute at least the max percentage they can match, that way you can get as much free money as possible!

It is important to note that if you want to be ambitious, you can contribute more than the employer match allows, experts recommend investing over ten percent. As previously stated, as of 2022, anyone under 50 years old can contribute up to $20,500 of their earnings to a 401(k) or 403(b), some of which can be matched by their employer. For a quick note, these numbers can change, depending on the economy for the year. For those over 50, they can contribute an extra $6,500 per year. This extra $6,500 is known as a **catch-up contribution,** which references how you can make up for the years where you did not save enough — usually when you are younger and might not know how to leverage your 401(k)!

Leverage your employer: IRAs

IRA stands for **individual retirement accounts**. This is more traditional than 401(k) and 403(b) plans. **Traditional IRAs** allow individuals to direct pre-tax income toward investments that can grow tax-deferred. **Tax deferral** is a term that refers to when a taxpayer can delay paying taxes until a certain point in time. For tax-deferred retirement accounts, taxes aren't withdrawn until you withdraw the money from your account in retirement.

A **Roth IRA** is a tax-advantaged individual retirement account that you can contribute to with after-tax dollars. This means that the contributions are not **tax deductible** — meaning, you cannot deduct those contributions from your taxes, but as soon as you begin withdrawing funds, the money is tax-free. This is especially a great option if your job does not offer a 401(k) or 403(b).

How do Roth IRAs compare to 401(k)s and 403(b)s?

The main categories of differentiation between the plans are how they vary in investment flexibility, tax contributions, retirement distributions, contribution limits, and employee matching.

- Investment flexibility:
  - » Roth IRA allows for greater overall control over your accounts, enabling your investments to grow for a longer period. It also provides a broader range of investment options, including stocks, bonds, funds, and more, and facilitates easier withdrawals.

» For 401(k)s, funds are limited to what your employer plan offers. Overall, there are fewer investment options compared to Roth IRAs.

» A 403(b) can only provide mutual funds and annuities.

- Tax contribution:

  » Roth IRAs have no tax deductions for contributions, but contributions can be withdrawn tax-free in retirement.

  » 401(k)s allow for a tax break if you contribute to your 401(k) plan. This is because you are able to deduct your contributions when you file your income tax return every year. Because you are subtracting your contributions from your taxes, this will save you money (and help you grow your net worth!)

- Retirement distributions: (Distributions is another term for withdrawals.)

  » Once you are already in retirement, your 401(k) requires you to take a required minimum distribution (RMD), which is the minimum amount you must withdraw every year from your 401(k). Because of this, you cannot leave all your money in your 401(k) when you are retired. If you do, you receive a 50% tax penalty on the RMD that was not withdrawn. All RMDs must be made by April 1st the year after you turn 72, or whenever you officially retire.

  » For the most part, you can withdraw your Roth IRA at any time or any age without any tax or penalty. You do not have RMDs, like 401(k)s.

» For 403(b), it is recommended that you do not distribute your funds until you are 59 years old because if you do so before then, half of your funds may be subject to taxes and early withdrawal penalties.

- Contribution limits

  » 401(k)s have higher contribution limits than Roth IRAs.

  » Roth IRA income limits have varied over the years, but the amount usually depends on how much you earned that year. Depending on how much you earn, the income limit can prevent you from contributing. In 2022, if you are single (as opposed to married) and have an income less than $129,000, you can make a full contribution to your Roth IRA. It would be reduced if it is between $1290,000 and $144,000. However, you will not be able to make a contribution to your Roth IRA if you make $144,000 or more. If you are married, these numbers are higher to account for your greater household income.

  » For 403(b)s, the limit for 2022 is $20,500. But if you are 50 years old or older, you can contribute another $6,500 as catch-up contribution (making a total of $20,500 + $6,500 = $27,000).

- Employer matching:

  » 401(k)s allow for employers to offer a match to your contribution to your 401(k) account.

  » 403(b) and Roth IRA don't allow for employer matching.

Across the three types of plans (Roth IRA, 401(k), 403(b)), which would you want as your own retirement savings vehicle, and why?

III. Cheat Code Recap

1. Retirement planning is the process of leveraging financial strategies of saving, investing, and distributing money to sustain yourself during retirement once your paid work ends.

2. Employee benefits are various types of non-wage compensation that employers provide to their employees in addition to their normal wages or salaries.

3. You can leverage plans including Across the Roth IRA, 401(k), and 403(b) to build your retirement savings.

Chapter 8
Investing

I. What is investing?

Investing often makes people feel behind or out of the loop. We frequently see images of wealthy men in suits frantically shouting "BUY!" and "SELL!" Or we think of Shark Tank—seriously, what do all of those words mean? And all of the sharks are literally millionaires who are super connected and have super successful businesses. So how can you even begin to understand it or get into it?

Let's break investing down to something closer to home. It can actually be thought of as studying. Usually, the more hours you put in, the higher of a grade you hope to get. However, we all know that this is not always the case. Sometimes you don't study at all or cram a couple hours before and ace a test, and sometimes you still fail after studying for hours on end. It sucks soooooo much when you put so much time and effort into studying just to get a bad grade. You did everything you needed to do on your part, but your grade didn't reflect that. Yet, it feels AMAZING when you ace a test you barely studied for! We know, though, that your odds of getting a better score if you study are higher, but, still, the odds are not always in your favor.

According to Investopedia, **investing** is the act of allocating resources, usually money, with the expectation of generating an income or profit.[81] You can invest in endeavors, such as using money to start a business, or in assets, such as purchasing real estate in hopes of reselling it later at a higher price.

II. Investing Principles

You might have heard the phrase: "Low risk, low reward. High risk, high reward." This gives us a simple clue about investing! Investing always includes risk, because regardless of how much research and/or money (or studying) you put in—there is never a 100% certainty that you will get a profit (or a good grade). Nevertheless, in general, the riskier something is, the higher the return is if it falls in your favor.

However, have you heard the phrase: "Don't put all your eggs in one basket?" This gives us another peak at effective investing strategies, specifically **diversification**. Essentially, to lower your risk of losing all or most of your money, it is helpful to diversify your investments.[82] Therefore, if one investment isn't looking too promising, some others might be fairing better—meaning not all your money will get lost.

Imagine you invested in both Zoom Video Communications (ZM) and AMC Holdings, Inc. (AMC). When the pandemic hit, movie theaters around the world had to shut down temporarily in response

---

81   Picardo, E. (n.d.). Investing explained: Types of investments and how to get started. Investopedia.

82   Segal, T. (n.d.). What is diversification? definition as investing strategy. Investopedia.

to COVID-19 restrictions, including AMC—likely reducing your investment value and causing losses. As a result, AMC's stock price dropped sharply in early 2020. On the flip side, Zoom's value surged as more people embraced remote work and learning, resulting in significant gains. Diversifying across different industries could help you maintain an overall positive return, unlike if you had solely invested in a struggling restaurant, where losses would likely occur.

III. Types of Investments

First thing to know is that there are many different types of investing. The three most popular types are:

- **Stocks**, also called **equity**, are securities (financial devices that can be traded and hold value) that give investors partial ownership in a company.[83] This ownership entitles the investor to a fraction of the company's profits and assets equal to the fraction of shares (units of stock) they bought. If the company is performing well, the value of the stock will show that. But if the company is being killed, the value of the stock will go down. The two main types of stock are:
  - » Preferred stock: Owners get first dibs on dividends (if the company allows) and repayment if the company goes out of business or is in a place to repay its investors with interest.

---

83   Hayes, A. (n.d.-d). Stocks: What they are, main types, how they differ from bonds. Investopedia.

» Common stock: Owners may receive dividends and the ability to vote at shareholder meetings. Common stock owners receive second dibs after preferred stock owners.

Pros & Cons:

- Pros for the investor: Higher risk, so higher potential return! Also, possible dividends!

- Con for the investor: Higher risk, so higher potential for loss.

- Pros for the issuer: Get funding to pay off debt, start new projects, and/or expand.

- **Bonds** are debt securities that can be issued by companies, principalities, and governments as fixed income securities.[84] Basically, the issuer of the bond has some debt they need to pay off, so they go to investors to help them out. A **fixed income security is** an investment where the investor is paid a fixed amount of interest periodically, and once the security reaches maturity, the issuer will receive the initial principal they paid in.

Pros & cons:

- Pros for the issuer: Pay off their debt

- Pros for the investor: Get their money back with interest in a fixed amount of time set by the issuer.

---

84   Fernando, J. (n.d.-a). Bond: Financial meaning with examples and how they are priced. Investopedia.

- Con for investors: A company can default on their bond (they do not pay you back the principal and/or interest payment), and you lose money.
- Pro/con: Bonds are considered low risk because they have lower returns compared to stocks and tend to be one of the safest investment vehicles in terms of not losing money.

- **Mutual Funds** are investment vehicles where investors contribute to a pool of money to build a big fund for professional investors and money managers to invest in diverse securities.[85] Diversification can be super hard to reach without a lot of dough, so mutual funds allow every dollar you invest to automatically be diversified! Investing in a mutual fund is very similar to investing in stocks because you own a share of the fund and are entitled to a fraction of the profit it generates.

Pros & cons:

- Pros to the investor: Shareholders may receive dividends and the benefits of a diversified portfolio.
- Pros to investors: Have a huge pool of money to invest with and receive fees from these funds.
- Cons to the investor: Usually have to pay fees to money managers for their services.

IV. How to invest BETTER than a professional

---

85   Hayes, A. (n.d.-d). Mutual funds: Different types and how they are priced. Investopedia.

It can be easy to confuse the everyday investor with the very well-paid professional trader who does it for a living. Their literal job is to trade securities, and they usually are MUCH more educated and trained than the everyday person, seeing as they probably went to school for it. Also, because it is their job, they have the time and knowledge needed to make decisions on these types of things.

It's important to note that it's best for the everyday investor to hold money in an investment account for as long as possible — the long game is the best game because compound interest will really work in your favor. Holding investments for a long time not only allows for compounding, but it means you don't have to fear when the market goes down. YouTuber The Money Guy Show thinks of investing like going up a mountain with a yoyo: the yoyo may be going up and down (like the market does in the short term), but in long term, you will reach a higher elevation than you did when you started. This is a notion that Warren Buffet would agree on.

Warren Buffett is known as one of the most successful investors of all time. His company, Berkshire Hathaway, owns over 60 companies, including Fruit of Loom (yes, the people who make undies), Dairy Queen, and even Geico. He has a net worth of over $95 billion! He has vowed to donate 99% of his wealth and also gives tons of advice to everyday investors.

Warren has often said, "Our favorite holding period is forever."

Don't try to time the market (buying and selling often/trading — what professional investors do). Buy and hold.

Did you know that professional investors actually suck at their jobs? Okay, maybe suck is a little harsh, but within the last 20 years, nearly 90% of actively managed funds (mutual funds that trade daily) did not beat the market![86]

The market, also known as the benchmark, is a combination of stocks and bonds — usually an index (a group of securities meant to imitate certain industries or the market in general) that is used to measure the performance of actively managed funds.

Index funds are mutual funds that are passively managed, meaning #NoTrading. Instead the securities chosen within the fund are a part of an index — not chosen by professionals, but automatically chosen based on if they fit the criteria of the index.

Index funds are sometimes known as an ETF (exchange-traded fund). A prime example of an index fund/ETF is the **S&P 500**. The S&P 500 is an index of the 500 largest US companies. Basically, it's how we know if professional investors who manage mutual funds are good at their jobs.

The fact that nearly 90% of professional investors fail to consistently outperform the market highlights that even those who are considered experts often struggle to achieve better results than a passive index fund strategy.

At Warren Buffet's annual meeting in 2020, he advised: "In my view, for most people, the best thing to do is own the S&P 500 index fund."[87]

---

86   Rosenberg, E. (n.d.). Most investment pros can't beat the stock market, so why do everyday investors think they can win? Business Insider.

87   CNBC. (2020, May 4). Warren Buffett: For most people, the best thing is to do is owning the S&P 500 index fund. CNBC.

According to Forbes, the best S&P 500 index funds of 2022 are:[88]

- Fidelity 500 Index Fund (FXAIX)
- Schwab S&P 500 Index Fund (SWPPX)
- Vanguard 500 Index Fund Admiral Shares (VFIAX)

All of these funds have very low fees and offer nearly identical (like, literally basically the same) returns. Both Fidelity and Schwab's have no minimum—so you can start no matter your budget. But Vanguard (which is still a great company—Buffett would agree) has a minimum of $3,000 to open. All are great options.

Buffet's Tips

Though index funds might be your best bet, maybe you want to live on the edge and try your hand at individual stocks and other investing options. Here are Warren Buffet's top tips to help you stay profitable:

1. **Invest by facts, not emotions!** Choose investments based on facts of how the company has been and is doing! You can actually find or listen to most companies' earnings reports online for free! So, make sure you do your research before choosing and not just how you feel a company will do or go with the crowd!

2. **Buy a wonderful business, not cigar butts.** Buffett advises that you should buy a wonderful business at a fair price and not a fair business at a wonderful price. You should buy a

---

88   Reeves, J. (2023, September 27). 5 best S&P 500 index funds of October 2023. Forbes.

company's stock at a price below its intrinsic value that you truly understand and know, at least factually, will do well.

3. **Only buy stocks that you understand.** When buying stocks, you should have a comprehensive grasp of what X company will look like economically in five to ten years. You should understand the company not just from the business side but also actively understand their customers' perspectives and experiences. And you should probably like it too if you're willing to invest in it!

4. **When you see a great opportunity, take it!** When it comes to investment opportunities, the time windows for best returns can be slim.

5. **Don't sell unless the business fundamentally changes.** Buffett highly recommends holding stocks forever! So unless there's a drastic change, take it to the grave!

V. The Bottom Line

Unfortunately, getting "rich quick" will happen for very few people (I know, we're sad too). We want to help you make the best decisions that stand the test of time, recessions, and pandemics. Of course, you can try doing things like picking your own stocks, trading, and investing in various securities (but make sure you make calculated decisions based on diligent research and use money that you are okay with losing).

VI. Cheat Code Recap

1. Investing is the act of allocating resources, usually money, with the expectation of generating an income or profit.

2. Diversification is an effective investing strategy to lower risk.

3. Different popular types of investment include stocks, bonds, and mutual funds.

4. Index funds are mutual funds that are passively managed.

Chapter 9
Insurance

I. What is insurance?

We get it ... insurance can be a confusing word with many different stigmatized and boring preconceptions. You probably think of the gecko from the Geico commercials explaining how "15 minutes can save you 15 hours on car insurance," or the Allstate guy explaining, "You're in Good Hands with Allstate," or even the State Farm commercial where the spokesperson says "Like a good neighbor, State Farm is there!"

For most people, this is probably one of the first things you think of when it comes to the idea of insurance. The commercials can be amusing, but the idea of insurance can sound gross and boring. BUT, understanding how important it is can be incredibly critical to helping you achieve financial independence and success!

Let's break it down for WHY exactly insurance exists and why it is important. The importance of insurance is that it de-risks the possibility of having to pay a large sum of money you don't have the means to pay.

The History

The idea of this actually roots back to *thousands* of years ago! The creation of civilizations brought on the idea of "community," and, because of this, the idea of protecting one another arose. Insurance can be dated back thousands of years, all on the founding principle that the strength of the community is just as important as the strength of the individual!

In your history class, you may have learned about *The Code of Hammurabi* (or maybe you will soon!). *The Code of Hammurabi* is known as the oldest code of laws in the world, used in Babylon, and it contains one of the earliest references of insurance![89] Specifically, in these laws, it is stated that if any member of the community is robbed, the community would band together and replace the stolen object.

So, whether it is someone stealing your ancient Babylonian valuables or even buying your first car or your first home, there always comes the risk that something might happen to those goods. They may break due to outside factors, like the weather. Or accidents may happen where you may cause damage, like rear-ending the car in front of you. Injuries are also a risk! While playing a sport, you may break your arm or leg — basically imagine everything in the commercials!

HealthCare.gov reports that it can be $7,500 to fix a broken leg.[90] If you get in an even worse accident, the average of a three-day hospital stay is around $30,000! And if you are terminally ill, it can

---

89   Beattie, A. (n.d.). The history of Insurance. Investopedia.

90   Health coverage protects you from high medical costs. Health coverage protects you from high medical costs | HealthCare.gov. (n.d.).

cost hundreds of thousands of dollars. Risk is everywhere in life, so insurance acts as a safety net when things don't go as planned.

When unexpected challenges arise, there is usually a cost—and in this case, literally a financial cost. You may need to repair damage to your car, replace expensive stolen items, or get surgery for an injury or illness. Those can really be incredibly expensive to pay for with your own money. Because of this, you have the option of hiring an insurance company to help.

How insurance works

As we mentioned, the purpose of insurance is to de-risk. It does this by having you pay insurance companies a smaller fee on a monthly basis, so that when you or your property get hurt, you don't have to pay a much larger fee. This is similar to a warranty on tech products that you can buy online. If you buy a TV or a gaming console, you might be able to opt in for a two-year warranty, for instance. The purpose of paying this small fee over time is, when in an emergency, your insurance company will pay for your bills because you are already protected under their agency. Thus, insurance companies are "financial intermediaries," meaning that they are a middle link between you and the companies you buy your goods or services from.

II. Why is insurance important?

Risk can be found anywhere, and accidents are incredibly common! According to the Bureau of Labor Statistics, a car accident happens every 13 minutes in the US, and the average driver will report a collision every 17.9 years. So, if you start driving at sixteen, you will likely be in at least one accident by the age of 34![91]

Anything valuable comes with risk, like the case of a car and the people who ride inside of it. High value also equals high risk. Owning valuables is an important step in growth, but theft and burglary are incredibly common, with the FBI stating that a burglary takes place every 30 seconds in the United States. What's even worse is, this number is an under-count. Oftentimes, marginalized communities are highly targeted in these types of crimes, and they go unreported.

Also, repairs and replacements are expensive! Take the car example: to replace an engine that is damaged during an accident would typically be anywhere from $7,000 to $10,000! And in the case of a car accident, a car accident of varying severity can cost you as "little" as $4.7 thousand to as much as $1.7 million![92] And if it is bad enough to the point that you need to call an ambulance, that is an additional $373 to $940, depending on the conditions and location.[93]

Frankly, these costs on their own are a LOT! And it is likely very challenging to be able to pay from your own bank account on short notice. Insurance is important because the unpredictability of life can mess up your goals so quickly! If you're saving for a goal but then break your leg — that's $7,500 gone! But what's even scarier (and more often the case) is, what if you weren't saving and broke your leg?

---

91   Motor Vehicle Safety Data. Motor Vehicle Safety Data | Bureau of Transportation Statistics. (n.d.).

92   Costs of motor-vehicle crashes. Injury Facts. (2023, April 12).

93   Pifer, R. (2022, February 22). Ground ambulance costs continue to soar, study finds. Healthcare Dive.

Later in this unit, we will be going over the following types of insurance to help you figure out ways to leverage it as much as you can to help you obtain your financial goals:

1. Life Insurance

2. Car Insurance

3. Health Insurance

4. Home Insurance

III. Choosing an insurance plan for you

Choosing insurance can feel overwhelming! There are so many different plans and possibilities, all with different benefits. The best way to navigate finding the right plan for you is to be honest about your financial situation and assess your current lifestyle. Are you adventurous? Do you drive often? How's your credit? Do you play a contact sport? There are many different types of options and online resources, such as LEMONADE, which will help you navigate various different types of plans!

If your employer offers insurance benefits, great! That's one thing taken care of. But you don't have to use employment plans! You should always compare the benefits your employer is offering to your state/federal marketplace.

If your employer does not offer insurance, then you can find your marketplace! You can begin by going to HealthCare.gov and entering your zip code. If your state has a specific marketplace available, you'll be taken to that one. If not, all good! You will use the federal marketplace to look for insurance. Usually, there are various types of tiered plans, where different options are mixed and matched so that you choose the type of insurance that is best for you.

Qualifications

When you send in your application for insurance, it can be as nerve-wracking as applying for a job or to a school! For health and life insurance, you have to provide basic information like your age, height, and weight. You will then be asked about pre-existing medical conditions, your medical history, and prescriptions taken.

After insurance companies review your application, the price of your monthly premium will change depending on your answers. For instance, if you have type 1 diabetes, and accurately report it, your health insurance premium will likely be higher for the company to take into account the extra risk associated with covering you. Some companies will even send a nurse to your home or workplace to verify your current health!

Putting the US into perspective

The **Affordable Care Act (ACA)** is a great example of how insurance works today in the US. The ACA operates with the goal of combatting long-standing issues in the US surrounding health insurance, primarily that 31 million people are uninsured and that health care is incredibly expensive in comparison to other countries.[94]

The biggest change that came from the ACA was that it is now required for many Americans to have health insurance, with a

---

94   Affordable care act (ACA) - glossary. Glossary | HealthCare.gov. (n.d.).

fee due if you are not insured. The ACA created health insurance marketplaces that acted to help people find affordable health care. These are all run by either the federal (national) or state government.

The ACA mandated that insurance companies cover preventative care — meaning check-ups at the doctors, shots, and blood tests must be paid for by the insurance companies. Also, they cannot require copayments — so you are paying for either half or a fraction of the service.

The ACA Gender Law works to combat the gender gap in payment. For instance, women pay much more for insurance than men because studies have shown that women face more potential risk, but this does not apply to companies with over 51 employees.[95]

IV. How to pay for insurance

If your job does not cover 100% of your insurance costs and/or you hire an outside insurance company, here are some methods for how you can pay for it:

Premiums

The amount you pay is called a "Premium", which is usually due monthly, but this can change from plan to plan. When paying for insurance, it is likely that you have two different ways of paying your premiums. The first is online, through your insurers website.

---

95   George, D. (2021, July 15). Why women pay more on average than men for auto insurance. The Motley Fool.

The second is through mailing, where you will mail a check to the insurers headquarters.

Explanation of Benefits (EOB)

An EOB is a statement sent from whichever insurance provider you chose explaining what services are covered by the company and what you might have to cover fully yourself or copay (when you pay a percentage of the cost, and the insurance company covers the rest). The provider will send this to you to help you better understand the value of your insurance. The EOB will be sent in the mail as a physical copy.

Electronic Remittance Advice (ERA)

ERA is a digital substitute made in place of a physical EOB and can be found online from your insurance provider.

V. Types of Insurance

Life Insurance

Life insurance protects against the risk of death — although a morbid thought, death is inevitable. Thinking about death is not fun, but the cost of death is often underestimated. There is sometimes a great financial burden that comes with paying for final expenses like a funeral (between $7,000 to $12,000). But what if you were financially supporting your family? Losing your income could force your family out of their home or abruptly change your family's way of life — and that's on top of grief!

Oof, we know, this is heavy. In a scene from an episode of The Simpsons, their TV displays, "Wifetime TV presents 'From Homemaker to Homeless,'" which gets an interesting conversation going. As these words are displayed, you can imagine the scene being reminiscent of a typical dramatic television show introduction. The phrase itself suggests a storyline where a character — specifically a homemaker — experiences a series of unfortunate events that lead them to lose their home and become homeless.[96]

Life insurance is meant to financially protect your family from the risk of your death. It can cover your funeral expenses as well as provide your family your missing income stream.

When we think about life insurance, we must first consider our current responsibilities and the number that is right for us. Do you have a family you support or are you single and living on your own? Those answers will affect the number your family would need and are unique to each person. For example, if the main breadwinner of a family of four were to pass, they might want to have a higher benefit amount than someone who only had one child.

Life insurance also should not be confused with a will. A will allocates the assets you already own to your loved ones, while life insurance, because of the nature of insurance, will pay out a monetary benefit that is more than what you paid into it.

---

96   IMDb.com. (2005, March 20). "Tthe Simpsons" mobile homer. IMDb.

Things to consider:

Generally

Life insurance premiums will vary based on your age, health, and lifestyle. Also, your gender will impact this! Generally, health insurance is higher for those who identify as female. This is because women live longer than men, and because generally women go to the doctors for preventative care more often.

Term vs Whole

There are two different types of life insurance out there.

- **Term life insurance** provides protection for a certain term (amount of years like ten or 30), usually has lower premiums.
- **Whole life insurance** provides protection until you die, usually much higher premiums with the added benefit of being able to use money you've paid in premiums after a certain point.

Race and Ethnicity

MOST people do not take time to think about the financial repercussions of death, but minority groups are especially at risk because they have less wealth to pay for an unexpected funeral or loss of income without life insurance. Also, life insurance agents get paid a commission based on the premiums they sell. Because of this, many life insurance agents will not even consider meeting with people who are low-income. This excludes not only most of America, but most minorities!

Tips & Tricks

Most professionals recommend getting a term life insurance policy because it is cheaper and, if you are investing/saving for retirement, you shouldn't need the cash value perk of a whole life plan.

Don't push it off! The older you get, the more likely you are to get illnesses and injuries that could hinder your ability to get coverage later on. Most insurance companies can't deny you coverage if you had a pre-existing plan with them! So getting life insurance in your young and healthy 20s might be the best move to have lower premiums and lock in your ability to get coverage!

Make sure you vet a few insurance agencies to see which one offers the best plan for you, and do your research on all of the products they recommend!

Health Insurance

Benefits

Whenever you get your first job, you can speak to your human resources department to find out about BENEFITS! Health insurance benefits are plans that are connected through your work, usually offering better deals and sometimes coming directly out of your paycheck, so you don't have to 1) worry about forgetting to pay that pesky premium and 2) save money using pre-tax dollars!

Medicare and Medicaid

Medicare and Medicaid are government programs that provide health and life insurance to specific underprivileged groups in the

United States. The US Department of Health and Human Services runs both programs from Washington DC.

Medicare covers hospital and medical care for elderly and disabled Americans! Those eligible are:

- People over the age of 65.
- People with physical disabilities.
- People with permanent kidney failure.

Medicaid covers medical care for low-income families and communities with limited resources. Medicaid can be supplemental, meaning that it can be added to a person's Medicare privileges, or to employer provided benefits! While Medicaid operates on the national level, each state is tasked with creating its own requirements. They will determine the duration of Medicaid, the scope of services offered, and the amount of money being used to support the cost of care.

Car Insurance

What it protects

As well as protecting your car from the risk of an accident, your car insurance can also protect you from paying for damages you cause to other peoples' cars and property. This type of coverage is called **liability insurance**, and it's required in most states. Also, **comprehensive coverage** protects you from events outside of your control. If a tree falls on your car or someone breaks your back window in an attempt to steal your car, your comprehensive coverage will cover the damage!

Home and Renters Insurance

Home and renters insurance protects your home from damages! When trying to qualify for a loan on your mortgage, you are required to have home insurance.

So, what are the different types of home/renters insurance?

There are three basic layers of coverage to your home insurance: replacement cost, actual cash value, and extended replacement cost/value.

- **Replacement Cost:** Without subtracting for depreciation (a loss in value due to use or damage), replacement cost coverage covers the expense of repairing or replacing damaged goods equal or similar to the cost you paid for it new.

- **Actual Cash Value:** This coverage replaces or repaid damage to and within your home, but it does subtract depreciation. Usually the cheaper option, depreciation is accounted for.

- **Extended Replacement Cost/Value:** This is an addition you can add to a replacement cost policy where, depending on the policy, up to 50% more value is added to your dwelling coverage (coverage on your physical home, not including the things inside it) for rebuilding.

Ultimately, your insurance type and the provider you choose will be specific to your own lifestyle and needs and will vary from person-to-person. What type of insurance and terms best match your needs?

VI. Cheat Code Recap

1. Insurance is important because risk is unavoidable and can be costly.

2. The Affordable Care Act (ACA) is US healthcare reform law aimed at improving access to health insurance and healthcare.

3. You can pay for insurance through premiums, Explanation of Benefits (EOBS), and Electronic Remittance Advice (ERAs).

4. Life insurance, health insurance, car insurance are some of the most common types of insurance.

Chapter 10
Taxes

I. Tax Basics

What are taxes?

When we hear anything about taxes, we have been socialized to learn that they are not a very exciting topic. But they are so important! We will do our best here to entertain you while teaching you what they are, why they are important, and how to go about them.

Taxes are a mandatory sum of money that must be paid and are charged by the local, regional, and national arms of government for public purposes.

Within our taxes, our tax revenues all go to public services, which are activities spearheaded by the government. This can include roadwork, opening and funding schools, providing social security, and/or healthcare insurance, and more.

But where do our tax revenues come from? This varies across different countries. For instance, in the US, the government often pulls most from individual income. This is known as **individual income taxes**. Meanwhile, other countries might rely more on other sources, like **consumption taxes**, which are taxes charged on goods and services.

But what does "filing your taxes" actually mean?

When we file taxes, we are completing our tax returns. A **tax return** is a form or a collection of forms that reports your income, expenses, and other relevant tax information (i.e. how much you have already paid in taxes for the year). They often must be filed annually. Your tax return allows for you as the person filing your taxes to (1) calculate your tax liability (how much you owe), (2) schedule tax payments, or (3) request refunds for overpaying any taxes.

In the US, we file our tax returns with the **Internal Revenue Service (IRS)**. The IRS is a government agency that is responsible for collecting taxes and enforcing tax laws in the US, and it was actually first established by Abraham Lincoln back in the 1800s! If you have any additional clarifying questions about any information in this chapter, we encourage you to refer to the IRS website at irs.gov.

So, why is it important to file your taxes?

Simply put, it is illegal if you do not. The government can claim civil or criminal penalties for you if you fail to file your return. More specifically, if you fail to file your taxes on time, you'll likely encounter what's called a Failure to File Penalty. The penalty for failing to file represents five percent of your unpaid tax liability for each month your return is late, up to 25% of your total unpaid taxes.[97] If you're due a refund, there's no penalty for failure to file.

---

97   Failure to file penalty. Internal Revenue Service. (n.d.-a).

Will you go to jail? No, in most cases, the IRS cannot actually send you to jail for failing to file your taxes. Also, if you are not able to pay the amount you owe because you do not have enough money, you will not be jailed.

Will you lose your home? The IRS does not want to make taxpayers homeless; however, they do need to collect the debt. They might recommend you sell your home in order to pay off your debt, or they might end up seizing it if they feel it is the only way to get paid. Just like the game of Monopoly, if you own a home, you can mortgage it!

It can often be easy to procrastinate on assignments and projects for school, leaving them to be done at the very last minute. However, one of the various things in life that we cannot procrastinate on are our taxes. However, it turns out that one-third (33%) of Americans file their taxes at the last minute.[98] Within this group of people, 40% report that filing taxes can be too time-consuming, 22% report it is too stressful, and 22% want to make sure they are filing it correctly, ten percent report that they doubt they will get a refund, and six percent report they are worried they will have to owe money.

If you are delayed in filing your taxes, you can file **Form 4868**.[99] This form is for any US individual who needs an automatic extension of their individual income tax return.

---

98   Tax Day 2021: America's biggest procrastinators. IPX1031. (2022, March 30).

99   Weltman, B. (n.d.). About form 4868: A 6-month extension to File your tax return. Investopedia.

II. What goes in your tax return?

Income

As mentioned in our previous unit, income is the money you are bringing in, often through work or investments. The most common way to report your income is by using a **Form W-2.**[100]

Form W-2 is known as the Wage and Tax statement. This is the document that an employer is required to send to each employee and the IRS by the end of the year. A W-2 reports an employee's annual wages and the amount of taxes that must be withheld from their paychecks.

Deductions

The Fun Stuff: How to Pay Less on Your Taxes, Part One!

Your tax deduction is what you subtract from your taxable income to lower the amount of taxes you owe to the IRS. How much you deduct usually varies depending on your region and your benefits. Oftentimes, you can deduct things like your retirement savings, alimony, and more. You can choose the standard deduction, or you can itemize your deductions on the section called Schedule A of Form 1040.[101]

Tax Credits

Next: How to Pay Less on Your Taxes, Part Two!

---

100   Team, T. I. (n.d.-b). Form W-2 wage and tax statement: What it is and how to read it. Investopedia.

101   About schedule A (form 1040), itemized deductions. Internal Revenue Service. (n.d.-a).

Tax credits are the total amount that offsets your taxes owed. This also varies across regions. Tax credits usually go to caring for dependent children, seniors, pensions, education, etc.

Once you report these three components on your tax return, the end of your return will show how much you owe in taxes or the amount of tax overpayment, which can roll over to the next year or be refunded. Just like taking care of debt or credit, you can pay it upfront in a single amount or pay it in installments over time.

III. What determines your taxes?

Throwing it back to the American Revolution, one of the biggest slogans was, "Taxation without representation is tyranny!" Back then, the Founding Fathers fought to make sure that the colonies would have a say in any tax policies put forth by the British government.

This was the case of the Stamp Act and the Townshend Acts, which were a series of tax policies that the British Parliament enforced in 1767.[102] During this time, they indirectly taxed goods imported to the American colonies — to make this more relevant, an example of indirect taxes today are sugar taxes levied on things like soda! However, at the time, the Founding Fathers ruled this unconstitutional because the colonies and the American people had no say in it.

Because of the Founding Fathers and the Constitution, we now have a say regarding taxes.[103] But as we mentioned, every region and every jurisdiction has a different tax policy. That means, who you

---

102   Independence Hall Association. (n.d.). The townshend acts. ushistory.org.

103   Beattie, A. (n.d.-b). Which amendment made income tax legal?. Investopedia.

nominate in politics matters at the local, regional, and federal level! With this, it may be less of a surprise to learn why it is still a big topic of controversy during election season.

IV. Different types of tax returns

There are various ways to file your tax returns with the IRS.

For individuals

If you are filing as an individual, you will use the IRS Form 1040 to file your annual income tax returns. Form 1040 asks for all individuals to disclose their taxable income for the year to determine whether they owe more taxes or if they will receive a tax refund. Oftentimes, the IRS requires you to file Form 1040 by April 15; however, in special scenarios, like during the COVID-19 pandemic, the IRS gave everyone an extension since so much was going on at the time.

Now, Form 1040 has been shortened to a two-page form thanks to the **Tax Cuts and Job Act (TCJA)**, which was a 2018 initiative made to improve the 1040 filing experience.[104] Yes, we approve of less pages!

Within these two pages, the IRS Form 1040 asks for the following information:

- Name
- Address
- SSN

---

104   Fontinelle, A. (n.d.). How the TCJA tax law affects your personal finances. Investopedia.

- Spouse and dependent individual information
- Whether or not you would like to contribute $3 to presidential campaign funds
- Wages
- Salary
- Taxable Interest
- Capital Gains
- Pension
- SSN benefits
- Other income types

Also, there are **standard tax deductions,** meaning if you make less than the standard deduction (below), you will get refunded all of the federal and state taxes that were taken from your gross income. Conversely, if your income exceeds the standard deduction, you'll still benefit as the taxes paid up to this standard amount can be refunded, effectively lowering your taxable income.

The standard tax deductions for tax year 2022 (to be filed in 2023) are as follows:

- Single or married filing separately, $12,950
- Married filing jointly or a qualifying widow(er), $25,900
- Head of household, $19,400

NOTE: Only use the standard tax deduction if the total of your itemized deductions and credits are below the standard deduction amount that applies to you.

There are additional types of Form 1040s, including the following:

- **Form 1040-NR:** This is a form for a various types of nonresident aliens (someone who has not passed either the green card test or the substantial presence test) who:[105]

  » Have engaged in trade or business in the US

  » Are representing a deceased person who would have had to file a 1040-NR

  » Are representing an estate or trust that have to file a 1040-NR

  You can find a sample of the 2021 1040-NR at www.fulphil. org/class-links and the most up-to-date year's form on the IRS website.

- **Form 1040-V:** This is a financial statement (we know what that is now!) that must come with a check or money order detailing the amount of taxes you owe. This provides the details behind the "Amount you owe" line of the 1040 or 1040-NR.

  You can find a sample of the 2021 Form 1040-V at www. fulphil.org/class-links and the most up-to-date year's form on the IRS website.

- **Form 1040-ES:** Those who usually file Form 1040-ES are individuals who are sole proprietors, partners, and S corporation shareholders—which is just fancy talk for self-employed or freelance. In these types of professions, you usually do not have

---

105　Block, H. (2023, January 10). What is a nonresident alien?. H&R Block®. https://www.hrblock.com/expat-tax-preparation/resource-center/filing/status/what-is-a-nonresident-alien/

taxes taken out of your pay before each paycheck. Instead, you file a 1040-ES and pay all the taxes you owe for the current year in a lump sum. This form is used to calculate and pay taxes for income that is not subject to withholding (e.g. self-employment, interest, dividends, rent, alimony). Often, it is filled out every **quarter**, which means you must pay **quarterly taxes** (every three months).

Every year has four quarters. The first quarter (Q1) is January 1st through March 31st; the second quarter (Q2) is April 1st through June 30th; the third quarter (Q3) is July 1st through September 30th; the last and fourth quarter (Q4) is October 1st through December 31st. The form does not need to be sent to the IRS but should be kept with your tax records for the year.

Pro-tip: If you meet the qualifications for the 1040-ES, it is probably a good idea to make sure you have money saved specifically to be able to pay these taxes when the time comes. Because taxes aren't being taken out of your income initially, it might be easy to spend that money on other things, or save it towards certain goals, only to not have enough or just be caught by surprise when Uncle Sam comes knocking for his money.

You can find a sample of the 2022 Form 1040-ES at www. fulphil.org/class-links and the most up-to-date year's form on the IRS website.

- **Form 1040-X:** This form is for those who might have made a mistake on their Form 1040 in the past.

You can find a sample of the 2021 Form 1040-X at www. fulphil.org/class-links and the most up-to-date year's form on the IRS website.

- **Form 1040-SR:** This is a newer form, specialized for seniors. It is the same as a normal Form 1040, but this version improves the experience. For instance, the form has a larger font and no shaded sections of pages to improve readability, in addition to additional deduction types just for seniors.

  You can find a sample of the 2021 Form 1040-SR at www. fulphil.org/class-links and the most up-to-date year's form on the IRS website.

- **Form 4868:** As mentioned, this form is for any US individual who needs an automatic extension of their individual income tax return.

  You can find a sample of 2021 Form 4868 at www.fulphil. org/class-links and the most up-to-date year's form on the IRS website.

For organizations: Corporations, LLCs, and Partnerships

Corporations are legal entities that are separate from its owners, according to Investopedia.[106] Corporations have many of the same rights and responsibilities as individuals, and that includes paying taxes. With this, corporations use **Form 1120**, which is catered to file federal income taxes.

---

106   Team, T. I. (n.d.-b). Corporation: What it is and how to form one. Investopedia.

LLCs (Limited Liability Corporation) also file the same form. LLCs are similar to a corporation, but LLCs have equity and corporations have shares of stock in businesses. LLCs have a more formal structure than partnerships.

Meanwhile, **partnerships** are another type of entity that also require filing taxes. Partnerships are formal arrangements by two or more parties to manage and operate a business. This means they share profits, and they share risks and losses. The difference between a partnership and corporations and LLCs is that partnerships issue percentages, as opposed to total amounts of stock. Oftentimes, professional groups in law, medicine, real estate, accounting, and more fields form partnerships. Partnerships use **Form 1065.**

V. Cheat code: The Totally Legal Tax Loopholes You Needed!

Trumping taxes: How the Wealthy Avoid Paying Taxes

Billionaire former President Donald Trump only filed $750 in taxes in 2016, the year he won the presidential campaign.[107] And in 2017, he filed $750 again! Based on what we've learned, that is FAR below what it should be. But how did he get away with it?

From his various businesses, Trump had significant losses, which he was able to roll over to help lower his income, and ultimately his taxes.

---

107   Jackson, D., & Subramanian, C. (2020, September 29). Trump says he still can't share returns after report he paid only $750 in income taxes in 2016 and 2017. USA Today.

Before his former Twitter account was officially banned, he tweeted, "paid many millions of dollars in taxes but was entitled, like everyone else, to depreciation & tax credits." One of his strategies was emphasizing his net operating losses. Trump accumulated at least a few billion dollars in losses a few decades ago and used that amount to save on his taxes until recently.

Knowing that billionaires like Trump can get away with not paying their taxes can truly be upsetting to those who really work for their money.

But as mentioned in Robert Kiyosaki's book, Rich Dad Poor Dad, "the rich don't work for money." This is one of the biggest takeaways from the book. Kiyosaki mentions that the poor and middle class often will pay more taxes than the rich will. This is because those who work for money will always be taxed the most.

Investing in assets

Individuals who have a high net worth often receive their income from assets. This can include things like stocks or investments. As these assets increase in value as the stock market increases, so does their total wealth. However, this income is not subject to tax, unless they sell their assets that create income. With this, they pay taxes whenever they sell their assets, which can really be any year they decide they want to sell.

Paying yourself a lower salary

To avoid a high tax rate, business owners with a high net worth tend to pay themselves lower salaries. For instance, Jeff Bezos of Amazon has paid himself $80,000 per year, while Apple founder Steve Jobs, former CEO of Hewlett-Packard Meg Whitman, Google cofounders Larry Page and Sergey Brin, and Facebook's Mark Zuckerberg all accepted an annual salary of $1 per year.[108]

To avoid this, politicians like Senator Elizabeth Warren, Senator Bernie Sanders, and President Joe Biden have proposed implementing a regular wealth tax to ensure that wealth, and not just income, would be taken into account.[109] Imagine how much these big-boss CEOs' taxes would amount to and how much can be done with that for public programs!

Relying on loans

Wealthy people often rely on loans to fund their lifestyles. They often borrow money from banks, which are more willing to lend it to them. As a result, the wealthy can also benefit from low interest rates, and their borrowed money does not count as income, so it is not taxable.

Hiring lobbyists and lawyers to help

For those who are super wealthy, they sometimes even go as far as hiring professional lobbyists, donate to lawmakers, and invest in policies that keep their taxes low.

Understanding the myriad ways in which the extremely wealthy navigate the tax system can be both enlightening and disheartening. The strategies they employ, from leveraging losses and depreciations

---

108   Morrell, A. (2014, April 1). Facebook's Mark Zuckerberg now among billionaire CEOS earning $1 salary. Forbes.

109   Schneider, H. (2019, October 17). Explainer: Democrats Warren and Sanders want wealth tax; economists explain how it works. Reuters.

to drawing income from assets and maintaining low salaries, highlight a complex interplay between wealth and tax policy. While such tactics may seem inaccessible to the average earner, they underscore the importance of financial literacy and the potential benefits of a more progressive tax system that could level the playing field. Proposals for wealth taxes aim to address these disparities, suggesting a future where public resources could be bolstered by contributions from those at the top. While the financial maneuvers of the wealthy may seem like a different world, they bring to light conversations about fairness and the structure of our tax codes—dialogues that are essential for a more equitable society.

How you can start

Based on an article in US News, they listed ways to reduce your taxes:[110]

1. **Contribute to a Retirement Account:** Your contributions to your accounts can be deducted from your taxable income. Because of this, it will decrease your federal tax returns.

2. **Open a Health Savings Account:** You will rarely and almost never get taxed if you spend your money on medical reasons. In fact, anything that goes to these types of accounts offer immediate tax deductions, grow tax-deferred, and can even be withdrawn tax-free.

3. **Check for Flexible Spending Accounts at Work:** Flexible spending accounts (FSAs) use payroll deductions to fund an account. This can be used to pay for expenses, ranging from

---

110   22 legal secrets to reducing your taxes | personal finance - US news. (n.d.-a).

insurance copays to over-the-counter medication. If you do not have a high-deductible health insurance plan, you can leverage your FSA to help you pay for your medical expenses tax-free.

4. **Use Your Side Hustle to Claim Business Deductions:** Whether you make candles or work on freelance projects, your business expenses can be tax-deductible. You can even write it off while you are on vacation, or deduct half of your self-employment taxes

5. **Claim a Home Office:** With remote working, this can be doable! In 2020 as a result of the COVID-19 pandemic, individuals could deduct $5 per square foot of their home offices, up to 300 square feet, for a maximum deduction of $1,500.

6. **Rent Out Your Home for Business Meetings:** You can file a tax claim on a portion of your rent.

7. **Get Credit for Higher Education:** According to the IRS, you can receive a tax credit of up to $2,500 of the cost of tuition, certain required fees, and course materials needed for attendance and paid during the tax year.

8. **See if You Qualify for an Earned Income Tax Credit:** This can be a refundable tax credit of up to $6,728 for 2021.

9. **Itemize Your Sales Tax:** If you make large purchases and your total sales tax payments are more than your standard deduction, you should itemize your sales tax. To do this, you must gather your receipts and figure out how much sales tax you've paid in total during the year. From this, reference Schedule A from Form 1040 and see if your state's standard tax deduction for

your income range. If your sales tax is higher than the state income tax, you can enter the total you've gathered from your receipt appropriately.

10. **Deduct Private Mortgage Insurance Premiums:** Once you own a home, you may be able to deduct several thousands of dollars annually in private mortgage insurance (PMI). This is a type of insurance you pay if you have a loan, which usually costs $30 to $70 every month for every $100,000 you borrowed. It is only possible to deduct when you itemize your deductions on the federal level.

11. **Make Charitable Donations:** You should be able to itemize your donations for up to $300 as a deduction.

12. **Adjust Your Capital Gains Tax:** Capital gains tax is a type of tax on the profit you earn from the sale of a non-inventory asset, like the sale of stocks, bonds, real estate, etc. If you invest, it is recommended to add in all reinvested dividends, which will increase your costs and reduce your capital gains. Meanwhile, for property and selling your home, you may pay capital gains tax if the value of your home has really increased a lot. You can be exempt for up to $250,000 for your home's appreciation, and double this if you are married, once every two years.

13. **Avoid Capital Gains by Donating Stock:** Ever wonder why people used to ask, "Can I pay you in Bitcoin?" The tax rates for cryptocurrency gains are the same as capital gains taxes for stocks. You can donate your stocks as if you were making a charitable donation.

14. **Invest in Qualified Opportunity Funds:** Qualified Opportunity Funds (QOFs) are created to help business and real estate investments towards low-income or economically distressed areas in the country. Investors can be incentivized by the government to contribute their money to the funds with the exchange of more lenient taxes. Charlamagne tha God and TI both do this!

15. **Claim Deductions for Military Members:** If you served in the military, you should be able to deduct any travel expenses that were not reimbursed.

16. **Consider State and Local Tax Breaks:** Every region can have different jurisdictions. In New York City, there is a parking tax for rented spaces of 18.375%, but it can be lowered by eight percent if you are a Manhattan resident and have your personal car parked in a long-term rented space for a month or more.

VI. Cheat Code Recap

1. Taxes are a mandatory sum of money that must be paid and are charged by the local, regional, and national arms of government for public purposes.

2. Filing your tax returns is mandatory, and the main components that go into it include your income, deductions, and tax credits. Tax return forms will vary based on the needs of varying individual and organization.

3. Wealthy individuals' taxes are lowered when they invest in assets, pay themselves lower salaries, and rely on loans.

Chapter 11
Credit

I. All About Credit

What is credit?

If we want to help you obtain the lifestyle you want—whether it's getting a loan for a car you are looking to buy or buying your first home—we can't do so without a conversation about credit.

Credit has a broad meaning and can also take on many different meanings when it comes to finance. According to Investopedia, credit is the contractual agreement in which a borrower receives a sum of money or something in value and repays the lender at a later date, generally with interest. Basically, one person borrows money from someone else, promising to pay it back, plus a little extra if it takes a while. Those who lend money are known as creditors, often individuals or entities such as credit card companies.

But how do we know how good our credit is? We often use credit scores to evaluate this. Your credit score is a number that reflects your reliability as a borrower, otherwise known as your creditworthiness. Basically, this is exactly what it sounds like—your credit determines if you are eligible or worthy. People also refer to it as "credit," for short.

What determines your credit?

Credit history is something that determines our credit scores. Lenders will often look at your credit history to understand your ability to repay debts to determine whether or not they should allow you to borrow their money. Credit history is documented in the form of a credit report. Credit reports provide full details of why your credit score is the way it is. This includes information on:

- How many accounts you've opened
- How long each account has been open
- How much you owe
- How much credit you have used
- How timely are you with paying your bills
- How many times you've had people look at your credit
- Who has looked at your credit
- Whether or not you have bankruptcies

However, it is important to note, credit reports are technically not "free." You are allowed to check your credit report once a year, but there are exceptions. This is because credit bureaus need to find ways to make money, so your credit report is considered a private record.

II. Why Is Credit Important?

The world economy runs on credit.

On a larger, more macro level, according to research, when you improve your credit, you as a consumer are able to borrow more money and spend more money. As a result of this, businesses can also earn more money and borrow and invest more (just like consumers!). When businesses borrow and spend money, it is oftentimes because they need more resources to support you and how they, as a business, can serve you and many others. Usually, this takes the form of hiring more people (yay, job creation!), and ultimately, creating more economic opportunity for communities. Really, our world economy operates on credit.

Credit helps you personally.

But on a more personal level, you can reap a lot of great benefits from having good credit! One of the biggest and main benefits of good credit is receiving lower interest rates.

Interest rate is defined as an additional charge to the amount you must repay your lender over the time you are borrowing their money. As time passes, your interest adds up, or compounds. This is known as compound interest. **Compound interest** grows when you earn interest on the money you save and the money you earn.

Here is an example to better understand compound interest:

Imagine you are hanging out with a friend, and your friend is looking to borrow some money for a meal because they forgot to bring their wallet. You choose to let them borrow $10 at a five percent monthly interest.

This means, by the end of the month, they must pay you $10, plus five percent interest:

5% of $10: $10 x 0.05 = $0.50

$10 plus 5% interest: $10 + $0.50

If they forget to pay you by this first month, you add another 5% onto that first amount, which is NOT $11 ($10.50 + $0.50).

Instead it would be 5% of $10.50: $10.50 x 0.05 = $0.52

So, by the end of two months, they would owe you:

$10.50 + $0.52 = $11.02

Okay, we know two cents isn't the end of the world, but it certainly becomes more serious when you are lending and borrowing more money. For instance, if you lended someone $10,000 to help them pay for their car with five percent interest, by the end of two years, this would actually be $11,050!

Because interest compounds over time, we obviously want to either pay people back sooner or have a lower interest rate. According to Experian, people with good credit usually receive lower interest rates.[111] A lower interest rate is offered because borrowers with good credit are more likely to pay lenders back on time. On the flip side, if someone has bad credit, it doesn't necessarily mean that they are not allowed to borrow money, but they are more likely to receive a higher interest rate — this is a way for lenders to offset risk.

---

111   Axelton, K. (2023, September 26). How does your credit score affect your interest rate?. Experian.

According to Forbes, some other perks of having good credit include (but are not limited to):[112]

- Having an improved likelihood of qualifying for a loan
- Receiving approval for certain jobs
- Getting larger credit cards and loan limits
- Receiving better credit card rewards
- Getting easier approval for rental properties
- Receiving lower insurance rates
- Avoid security deposits on utilities
- Have more negotiating power on loan terms

III. Types of Credit

Now that we understand why credit is important to build, it is important that we understand the different types of credit before we go into how to improve your credit.

Here are the different types of credit and how they can each impact your credit score and creditworthiness:

Installment Credit

Installment credit is a loan of a fixed amount that you make specific payments toward over a set period of time, often months or years,

---

112   VanSomeren, L. (2023, September 7). 9 benefits of good credit and how it can help you financially. Forbes.

until the loan is paid off.[113] Also referred to as **closed-end** and **non-revolving credit.**

Installment loans can also come with origination or late fees.

- According to Investopedia, **origination fees** are a type of fee that is made to a lender for processing the loan application.[114] These are upfront fees aside from the loan itself. The typical origination fees are a percentage of the total loan, and they can usually range between 0.5% to 1% of a mortgage loan in the US. Sometimes, they are also called discount fees or points.

- **Late fees** are a type of charge that consumers must pay when they make a late payment—exactly what it sounds like. Late fees can vary depending on who is missing them. For instance, some late fees can be an additional $20 charged for every 30 days they are behind schedule, or you can charge three percent for every 30 days they are late. For this latter case, it works similarly to interest.

Installment loans typically include:

- Mortgages
- Car loans
- Personal loans
- Credit accounts

---

113   McGurran, B. (2023, May 15). What is installment credit?. Experian.

114   Kopp, C. M. (n.d.). Origination fee: Definition, average cost, and ways to save. Investopedia.

Revolving Credit

Imagine a revolving door. It can never really close as long as it's working and turning. That is similar to the idea of revolving credit. It is always "open" — you are always able to see your credit. Also, when you are walking through a revolving door, it allows you to use it while someone is simultaneously walking out the other way. There is constant motion in both directions.

Revolving credit works in a similar way. **Revolving credit** is a type of credit that allows you to borrow, with the condition that you repay a portion of the current balance in regular payments, even if the full amount borrowed has not been entirely paid off. There is also no specified end date; it is always open as long as you are in good standing. It is also often called **open credit** or **open-ended credit.**[115]

For revolving credit, lenders will set a **credit limit.** A credit limit is the maximum amount that you can have charged to your account and are able to borrow. So, when you buy something with your credit, you will have less available credit remaining until you make a payment.

However, if you fail to make the payment for the minimum balance you owe every month, the unpaid portion carries over to the next month. This idea is known as revolving balance. Imagine if someone was using a revolving door and didn't get out in time. They have to keep going until they get their turn, the next time they see the exit!

If you have a higher revolving balance, you will also have more interest the next time you will be charged, on top of the amount that has carried over. So, it is important that you pay the minimum amount needed every month.

---

115   Bankrate. (n.d.). The difference between revolving and nonrevolving credit.

Some types of revolving credit accounts include:

- Credit cards
- Personal line of credit (basically, a credit card)
- Department store credit cards
- Service station credit cards
- Overdraft protection for checking accounts
- Bank-issued credit cards
- **Home equity line of credit (HELOC)**
  - » Home equity is equal to your home's value minus your balance owed (like your mortgage).
  - » HELOC is a revolving credit with a maximum loan amount of your home's equity

With these types of accounts, you are likely to be charged a monthly or annual fee for keeping the account open. Meanwhile, you may also be more tempted to spend money/credit on things that might not be necessities. For instance, if you open a line of credit under a department store credit card (e.g. Apple, Uber, Disney, Gap, etc.), you are more likely to opt in for purchases with those companies.

At the end of the day...

It is important for you to make an effort to diversify your credit, just like how investors would diversify their portfolios. By doing so as a borrower, you will be able to show lenders that you can responsibly manage various types of credit. If you were to imagine the flip side, if you were a lender, you would want to make sure your money is safe with your borrower and de-risk the process as much as possible. To know that your borrower can manage different types of credit well can be very reassuring.

Credit Cards

With all this talk about credit, your mind is probably now wondering about credit cards. What are they? Where do you get them? Why do so many shows on TV show someone spending recklessly on credit cards?

It is important for us to first explain the concept of credit before you understand credit cards and why they exist. Often on TV shows, you will see a character getting their first credit card and spending it recklessly because they don't have to spend their own money upfront. Imagine, if you didn't understand the idea of credit and debt, this sounds pretty magical! However, there always comes a point in the TV show episode where that character realizes that they owe the money back.

And if they don't pay it back quickly, that amount grows over time (no thanks to interest and late fees!).

The early history of credit cards

There are theories that the ways of exchanging money in a "valueless" way has its roots in ancient Mesopotamia, where people used clay tablets to keep track of how they exchanged goods.[116] These clay tablets were utilized because they were easier to use than having to go through the intense process of producing lots of copper coins.

---

116   The history of credit cards. CreditCards.com. (2023, May 8).

This method continued to be used in the 1800s, where merchants and farmers used credit coins and charge plates as a way to provide some time before merchants would collect profits from the farmers' harvest.

In 1950, The Diners Club card launched from an incident where a man named Frank McNamara forgot his wallet and was unable to pay for his business dinner. Frank proposed the idea of creating a small cardboard card for those who can charge an amount of money on it and pay the full amount by the end of the month.

In 1958, American Express launched their first credit card made of cardboard. The year after, in 1959, they made the first plastic credit card.

Revolving credit — which we now know is a type of credit that allows you to borrow, with the condition that you are repaying a portion of the current balance in regular payments — was then introduced. Bank of America/Visa and Mastercard then become some of the biggest credit card systems, afterwards in the 1960s.

Before Visa and Mastercard arose, consumers did not have to choose where they kept their lines of credit. Initially, this was known as a closed-loop system. But with more bank cards arising, they were forced to choose.[117] This made things complicated, so bank card associations allowed an open-loop system that allowed for interbank cooperation and transfer of funds.

From then onwards, the growth and innovation around credit cards became a fast-paced field. This caused various laws to be

---

117   Hayes, A. (n.d.-f). Visa vs. Mastercard: What's the difference? Investopedia.

introduced, including the Fair Credit Reporting Act of 1970, the Fair Debt Collection Practices Act of 1977, and more.[118]

As time passed, more technological advances were made to credit cards, including adding magnetic strips (allowing you to slide your card on the scanner), microchips (allowing you to dip one side of your card into the scanner), and even radio-frequency identification (RFID) (allowing you to tap your card or even your phone on the scanner).

A lot has happened in the world of credit cards in the past 70+ years, and there is still so much more technological transformation that is yet to come.

How to get and choose a credit card

Technically, anyone aged 18 and up can apply for a credit card.[119] The main requirements that you must provide are your legal name, birth date, social security number (SSN), and annual income.

Some credit card companies require you to have an independent income or have a co-signer, especially if you are anywhere from 18 to 20 years old. A co-signer is another person who agrees to also have responsibility for the charges that are made to that credit card. Your co-signer can even be 18, but oftentimes, it may be likely that another 18-year-old might not have enough financial resources, credit history, or job history to be a creditworthy co-signer. Regardless, having a co-

---

118   Kenton, W. (n.d.-a). Fair debt collection practices act (FDCPA): Definition and rules. Investopedia.

119   Crail, C. (2023, May 15). How old do you have to be to get a credit card?. Forbes.

signer is often a way to build good credit and increase your chances of getting approved for the card.

Every credit card has different perks and terms. Here are some factors worth considering when you are figuring out which card is best for you:[120]

- **Annual Percentage Rate (APR)**: This is the cost of borrowing the card if you don't pay the entire balance off by the end of each month. Basically a fancy word for interest rate.

- **Minimum repayment:** If you do not pay off your balance by the end of each month, you must pay a minimum amount. This depends on your bank. It can be a small percentage of whatever balance is due, or a specific fee, like $25.

- **Annual fee:** This is the fee you are charged each year just for using it. Lower fees are better! This fee is added to the total amount you have due.

- **Charges:** This includes late fees, fees for overspending your credit limit, or fees for charging your credit card for international purchases. Apple's Credit Card is known for having no annual fees, foreign transactions, or late fees.

- **Interest rates:** As we defined earlier, interest rates are additional charges to the amount you must repay your lender over the time you are borrowing their money.

- **Loyalty points and rewards:** Like many fun things, credit card companies like to gamify things. They incentivize you to make purchases based on a points and rewards system. Let's look

---

120   Choosing and applying for a credit card. Citizens Advice. (n.d.).

at Starbucks for example. For every dollar you spend with a Starbuck Visa card, you will be able to earn two stars to your loyalty card. On the other hand, if you use Starbucks loyalty card (not the credit card, but the regular account), you get only one star per dollar spent. If you are a big coffee drinker and like your morning Starbucks, this could be a neat card for you. There are other cards that offer points and rewards systems on travel programs, as well. At the end of the day, different credit cards have different point systems.

- **Cash back:** Cash back is where you get your money refunded to your card based on how many points and rewards you accumulate. This is a way to earn money back on your purchases, and it's a good perk for anyone who can pay off their bills in time, in full, every month. If you do not pay it off quickly, this will hurt your credit score.

Try applying this. Compare the different types of credit cards. Based on your findings, which is best fit for your personal habits and lifestyle?

On the other hand, if you are under 18, there are still ways that you can build your credit while in high school to help you be a better candidate once you actually apply for a credit card! This includes some of the following:

- **Open a checking and savings account.** You can open a checking account at the age of 13! The condition is that your parents/ guardians must be co-signers. Once you turn 18, you may get your own checking and savings accounts. Even though checking and savings accounts don't really impact your credit score, these accounts are still the foundation of how you manage your finances, which can help you build good habits to build your credit score.

- **Become an authorized user on your parent's card**. This can help you build your own credit history. However, it is important to make sure that they have good credit history. If they do not have a good credit history, this will negatively affect your credit score.

- **Get a secured card.** When you turn 18, you can also apply for a secured credit card. This is not a traditional credit card. Secured credit cards are made for people who are just starting to build their credit and don't have enough history yet.

A word of caution against credit cards

As Spiderman's Uncle Ben said, "With great power, comes great responsibility." Credit cards are one of those things that this seriously applies to!

Using credit cards is a serious responsibility that demands strategic planning and disciplined spending. Building a good credit history is essential, as it influences many aspects of financial life. It's vital to use credit cards within your means; otherwise, the repercussions can extend beyond financial strain. Poor credit management can lead to higher interest rates on loans and can make it more challenging to obtain a mortgage or car loan. It might even impact your rental applications and, in some cases, employment opportunities. While the dire consequence of bankruptcy is a distant possibility, it's the accumulation of smaller setbacks — like increased payment requirements and damaged credit scores — that can incrementally strain personal relationships and financial health.

According to Investopedia, you should be cautious of the following points before you decide to commit to applying for a credit card:[121]

- Credit cards can discourage self-control on spending and encourage impulsive buying habits.

- Credit cards are not good if you do not have a good handle on your budget. With credit cards, it can be easier to charge purchases without as much thought.

- Interest builds up over time if you don't keep an eye on it.

- Your APR, which starts at a lower percentage, can go up VERY quickly if you do not pay off your balance in full.

- Having bad credit is harmful for your insurance, job opportunities, and real estate endeavors, whether it's renting, buying, or refinancing your home.

- Being in debt puts stress on other loved ones around you.

- If you are not careful, you can go bankrupt. It is much more serious in real life than losing a game of Monopoly!

IV. How to Improve Your Credit

- Keep your credit card balances low. Your credit utilization ratio is a proportion that tells how much available credit you are

---

121   Fontinelle, A. (n.d.-a). 9 reasons to say no to credit. Investopedia.

using at any given period of time. It is sometimes also called a revolving utilization (recall revolving credit!). You can calculate it by dividing your total balances across all your accounts by your total credit limit. If you use more than 30% of your credit, this can be seen as a red flag to lenders.

- Pay your bills on time. If you pay your bills on time, you can also benefit from cash back depending on your credit card!

- Pay more than the minimum amount you are asked to pay (especially for revolving credit)

- Consider paying off higher debt accounts first. These accounts with high debt usually have higher interest rates. We want lower interest rates!

- Do not close accounts unnecessarily. Sometimes, this can lower your credit because it lowers the average age of accounts on your credit report.

- Check your credit report often. It is recommended to check your credit reports frequently to see why your credit is the way that it is. If, for some reason, you are seeing information that does not reflect your spending and borrowing habits, you need to raise a concern because you may be victim of identity theft, which is when someone uses your personal information (name, ID, credit card number, etc.) without your permission to commit fraud or other crimes. We don't want that!! So, make sure you are checking your information often and be careful about how you communicate any personal information. Plus, it also turns out that if you fix an error on your credit report, you can also improve your credit score.

- Spend responsibly: This is a basic rule of thumb, but it should never be understated!

V. Cheat Code Recap

1. Credit is the contractual agreement in which a borrower receives a sum of money or something in value and repays the lender at a later date, generally with interest.

2. Interest rate is defined as an additional charge to the amount you must repay your lender over the time you are borrowing their money. As time passes, your interest adds up, or compounds. This is known as compound interest. Compound interest occurs when you earn interest on the money you save and the money you earn.

3. There are different types of credit, including installment credit and revolving credit.

4. You can improve your credit by: keeping your credit card balances low; paying your bills on time; paying more than the minimum amount you are asked to pay; considering paying off higher debt accounts first; not closing accounts unnecessarily; checking your credit reports often; and spending responsibly.

Chapter 12
Banks

I. Bank basics: What is it and why does it exist?

Why do we even have banks?

When we think of banks, we often think of a safe place to hold money. The first bank was created in Philadelphia by inspiration of Alexander Hamilton. If this name sounds familiar, it probably is — think of the same Hamilton from Lin-Manuel Miranda's Broadway hit play!

Alexander Hamilton's financial strategy was foundational in shaping the early economic framework of the United States. His plan to pay off over $75 million in national debt was aimed at stabilizing the nation's finances and establishing robust credit for the government. By assuming state debts and centralizing financial control, Hamilton intended to improve the nation's creditworthiness, thereby fostering trust in the government's ability to manage business and economic affairs. This move was also designed to encourage investment and create a predictable environment for commerce and industry, setting the stage for economic growth and development. Since then, banks have continued to play very important roles for society, whether it's paying off the government's debt from the Revolutionary War to helping you get the loan you need for your tuition!

Banks have many roles, but their main function is facilitating the borrowing and lending process.[122] This means that they: (1) take in funds from those who have money, (2) act as a safe intermediary exchange, and (3) lend that money to others who might need it.

In this case, those who have money and are giving it to the bank are called **depositors**. They are often individuals, households, financial and nonfinancial institutions, and local or national governments. So, when you deposit money into your bank account, that means you are giving it to the bank as well as storing it somewhere safe.

Bank services

Banks today offer various services. Aside from opening and closing accounts, or facilitating deposits and withdrawals, other types of bank services include:

- **Wealth management:** This is often a service that combines general financial services to help provide advice to banks' more well-off clients. This usually begins with financial advisors asking details about their customer's specific situation and goals. The financial advisor then creates a game plan for that individual to obtain their financial goal. Often, their topics of conversation around wealth management are related to investing, real estate, accounting, retirement, and tax services.

---

122   Jeanne Gobat is a Senior Economist in the IMF's Monetary and Capital Markets Department. (2017, June 15). Banks: At the heart of the matter. IMF.

Wealth management, however, does not come for free—which is why wealthier people tend to leverage this service. Usually, the bank charges these clients based on his or her **assets under management (AUM)**, which is essentially the total value of assets that an individual manages. Typically the rate is around one percent or more of the clients' AUM, depending on the bank.

- **Currency exchange:** If you are traveling to and from a different country, you likely will not have the same currency. You can't use pesos, pounds, or yen in the US—they are not the same as a US dollar, nor do they have the same value. With this, you can usually go to your bank to exchange currencies. Banks will charge a fee for every exchange. The fee will vary, as it often depends on which bank you go to. Nevertheless, it is almost always cheaper to exchange currencies at a bank here in the US than at foreign airports.

- **Safe deposit boxes:** A safe deposit box is a secure container that is used to store valuable assets at a bank or credit union. This can be cash, jewelry, contracts and important papers, physical stock, or anything that is of prized value. Some banks, however, do not allow storing cash and are strict on the types of items you are allowed to store. Banks usually charge a fee for safe deposit boxes, as well. The fees here also vary depending how big of a storage space you are looking for.

Types of banks and systems

There are four types of banks that you should familiarize yourself with:

- **Retail banking:** Retail banking is a type of banking we might be more personally familiar with. It provides financial services to individuals, as opposed to businesses.[123] This is why it is also sometimes called **consumer banking**. Retail banking functions to help individuals manage their money, access and build their credit, and deposit their money safely. Retail banks also offer onsite customer service to provide financial advising for their customers. There are also various types of retail banks that vary in size, whether they serve a local community or a larger, more global, corporate scale. The largest and most-used retail banks as of 2021 are JPMorgan Chase, Bank of America, Wells Fargo, Citibank, and US Bank.

- **Credit unions:** Credit unions often provide better interest rates for their clients because they are not corporate entities seeking profits, and, as a result, are not required to pay corporate taxes on earnings. Technically, credit unions are not banks. A bank is a for-profit financial institution while a credit union is a non-profit financial institution, although credit unions offer similar types of services. Credit unions are often also known for better customer service and lower fees.

- **Commercial or corporate banking:** Corporate banking is a type of banking that strictly serves companies. The companies can be

---

123   Majaski, C. (n.d.). Retail banking: What it is, different types, and common services. Investopedia.

of any size, no matter how small or large. The financial worth of transactions is often higher for corporate banking than in retail banking, which makes sense as businesses deal with greater amounts of money than an individual would by themselves. Corporate banks function to provide a range of services to businesses, including loans and other credit products, treasury and cash management services, equipment lending, commercial real estate, trade financing, and employer services.

- **Investment banking:** Investment banking is a special segment of banking operation that helps individuals or organizations raise capital and provide financial consultancy services.

II. The US Banking Structure

The Federal Reserve (Fed)

Ever wonder where the government got all the money for stimulus checks? The Fed is an abbreviated term that stands for Federal Reserve. The Federal Reserve is the central bank of the United States. They oversee everything, from managing inflation and regulating all aspects of banking on an international level to managing the supply of US dollars in national circulation.

The Fed was founded by Congress in 1913 to provide the nation with a central and reliable financial system.[124]

---

124   Federal Reserve Education. (n.d.).

By establishing the Fed, the US was divided into 12 geographical districts with separate Reserve Banks. The 12 districts are only one of the three segments of the Fed.

There are three key groups that make up the Federal Reserve System:

- The Board of Governors
- The Federal Reserve Banks (Reserve Banks)
- The Federal Open Market Committee (FOMC)

Collaboratively, these three entities make decisions that help promote the health of the US economy and the stability of the US financial system.

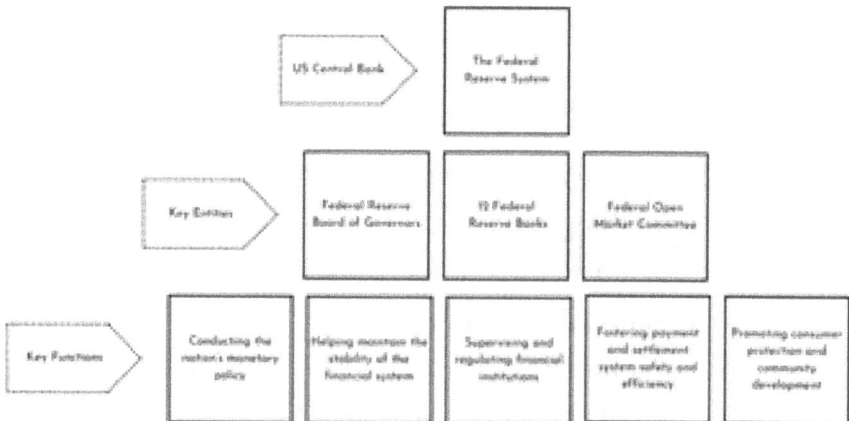

III. An Unequal World of Banking: The Unbanked

The **"unbanked"** population refers to individuals who do not have a traditional bank account or access to mainstream financial services, such as savings and checking accounts, credit cards, or loans, through a regulated financial institution. Instead, the unbanked relies on alternative financial services, cash transactions, and informal methods for managing their finances. As a result, the unbanked population often faces financial exclusion, limited access to credit, and barriers to participating fully in the formal financial system.

According to the 2021 National Survey of Unbanked and Underbanked Households by the Federal Deposit Insurance Corporation (FDIC), over six percent of US households are unbanked.[125] That is 14.1 million American adults!

The racial wealth gap is especially prominent here. Black (16.9%) and Hispanic (14%) households are around five times as likely to be unbanked compared to White households (3%). But why?

The biggest factor that influences the unbaked are their levels of income. An average of approximately 19% of households with a household income of less than $30,000 are unbanked. Meanwhile, 2.4% of unbanked households earn more than $30,000 per year.

If the unbanked population lacks access to the needed financial services, they must resort to other options for making regular transactions. This can vary from cashing checks, saving money, borrowing money, etc.

---

125   Economic inclusion. FDIC. (n.d.).

However, these other options have lots of risk that the unbanked population is typically unaware of. For instance, being unbanked and leveraging alternative options can lead to them going to predatory lenders, paying inflated interest rates, or having to live paycheck-to-paycheck.[126] In the long run, this is financially unsustainable. Retirement planning is no longer a viable or accessible option, either.

Why don't the unbanked use the bank?

Now, you are probably wondering, if being unbanked has so many negative consequences, why don't some people use the bank? Here are some of the top drivers:

1. **The unbanked feel distrust in and are often worried about banks' high overdraft fees.** According to a survey conducted by Pew Charitable Trusts, 72% of respondents reported they prefer alternative and prepaid cards over traditional banking services because they were trying to avoid overdraft fees.[127] You are probably wondering what the fees typically are? According to the Consumer Financial Protection Bureau, banks make a total of $11.2 billion in fees from overdraft fees and penalties.[128] That is a really big number, so it makes sense why people can be fearful of that!

   As a result, according to Mehrsa Baradaran's How the Other Half Banks: Exclusion, Exploitation, and Threat to Democracy,

---

126   Hayes, A. (2023, May 23). Predatory lending: How to avoid, examples and protections. Investopedia. https://www.investopedia.com/terms/p/predatory_lending.asp

127   Banking on prepaid report - the pew charitable trusts. (n.d.-c).

128   Stein, G. (2016, February 25). New insights on bank overdraft fees and 4 ways to avoid them. Consumer Financial Protection Bureau.

it turns out that some banks even removed some of their bank branches from low-income communities.[129] This is a huge problem of accessibility, especially with individuals or families who have no cars or free time to commute to their bank, or in communities with little to no public transportation services. This is how cash goes under the mattress and can lose value over time.

2. **The unbanked feel distrust in banks because they are also businesses.**[130] At the end of the day, banks are also businesses that are trying to make money. Just like any other business, the goal of a bank is to earn a profit for its owners and shareholders. Banks do this by charging more interest on the loans and other debt they issue to borrowers than what they pay to people who use their savings vehicles. Like businesses might fail, if a bank fails, you lose your money in that bank.

    This underlying skepticism towards banks can also be traced back to historical events where the failure of financial institutions had dire consequences for the average citizen. Notably, during the 2008 financial crisis, numerous banks faced insolvency due to overexposure to high-risk mortgages, leading to the collapse of savings for many working and middle-class individuals. The government stepped in with massive bailouts to stabilize the financial system, yet the crisis left a lasting impact on public

---

129   Baradaran, M. (2018). How the other half banks: Exclusion, exploitation, and the threat to democracy. Harvard University Press.

130   LaMagna, M. (2016, September 23). 10 million US families don't use a bank - here's what it costs them. MarketWatch.

confidence. This event is a stark reminder that while federal insurance programs now protect individual depositors up to a certain amount, the health of the banking system is intrinsically linked to the financial security of its customers.

3. **The unbanked feel cultural stigma in banks.** Oftentimes, immigrant and minority populations do not like going to the bank because their grasp of the local language is not very strong. Imagine if we sent you to a foreign country to set up a bank account and fill out paperwork in a language you were unfamiliar with — that is SO uncomfortable, and it is understandable why there is a big barrier!

It is unfortunate that there are so many barriers for those who are more prone to be unbanked. In the long term, this can be harmful for a number of reasons, including some of the following:

- **They might be unprepared for emergency situations, which might require them to take a loan.** But individuals without a bank account, securing a loan in emergency situations can be particularly challenging. Without the traditional banking relationships that facilitate credit checks and loan approvals, they may have to seek alternative lending sources. These might include payday lenders, title loan companies, or pawn shops, which often charge significantly higher interest rates compared to traditional banks. This can create a cycle of debt that's hard to escape. During the COVID-19 pandemic, the difficulties of obtaining emergency funds without a bank were highlighted. Many relief measures, including stimulus payments and expedited loans, were distributed through banking channels, which meant that the unbanked faced additional hurdles to access much-needed financial support. This underscores the importance of financial inclusion as a means of ensuring that all citizens have access to essential financial services during crises.

- **It is hard to build credit history and build wealth without having an account with a bank.** A bank account is often the first step in establishing a financial record that credit reporting agencies use to generate a credit score. Regular transactions and account history through a bank provide proof of financial stability and responsibility, which are critical when applying for credit cards, loans, and even rental agreements. Without these, lenders and businesses have no financial behavior to assess, making it difficult to obtain credit or favorable terms. Additionally, bank accounts often provide access to financial services such as savings accounts, which can earn interest, and investment products that can help grow wealth over time. Without these tools, individuals may miss out on opportunities to build their financial future and may have to rely on costly alternative financial services that can hinder wealth accumulation.

- **They might not have much savings.** Out of all the unbanked households that are actively saving, many store their savings through informal, and insecure, ways. This can include storing cash at home, with family, in pre-paid cards, or other alternatives that do not earn interest, are subject to fees, and will depreciate over time.

IV. Opening a Checking or Savings Account

Overall, there are many benefits to opening up a bank account. Here, we'll provide some basic steps that can guide you to do so. But overall, if you go to your local bank, there are usually bankers there who can be very helpful with the process and essentially do all the work for you on the spot. If you or someone you know might be hesitant due to language barriers, it can be helpful to find a bank with a translator or bring a family member or friend with you to help translate the necessary information.

Here are the main basic steps it takes to open an account:

1. To open a checking or savings account at a bank, you will need a minimum amount to make your first deposit. This depends on the bank you end up using. For some, it can be as little as $1! Don't go to the first bank you see, though. Try to get a lay of the land and compare different banks near you with each other.

2. Come prepared with identification to prove you are the person you say you are!

   For US Citizens, you'll need to provide identification such as your:

   - Social Security Card
   - Birth Certificate
   - Passport
   - Driver's License
   - State Identification Card

Meanwhile, for non-US Citizens, you will need to come prepared with any of the following:

- Foreign Passport with Photo
- Foreign Driver's License with Photo
- Foreign State-Issued ID
- Employment ID with Photo
- College ID with Photo
- Alien Registration Card with Photo
- Permanent Resident Card with Photo

3. Fill out a questionnaire to answer some more specifics about your background.

4. Set up your bank login and PIN! With banks having online platforms, you will be provided a login to be able to see your financial health online, as opposed to having to go into the bank in person. Meanwhile, your PIN is your 4-digit passcode you must remember and keep private! You will use this number to approve transactions

5. Make a deposit. This can occur in a variety of different forms, and every bank has its own instructions for how to do so

- In-person
- ATM
- Online
- By Mail
- Direct Deposit
- ACH

V. Cheat Code Recap

1. The main function of banks is facilitating the borrowing and lending process.

2. Common types of banks and systems include retail banking, credit unions, commercial or corporate thinking, and investment banking.

3. The Federal Reserve is the central bank of the United States, and it oversees everything, from managing inflation and regulating all aspects of banking on an international level to managing the supply of US dollars in national circulation.

4. The "unbanked" population refers to individuals who do not have a traditional bank account or access to mainstream financial services due to different factors, including general distrust in banks.

Chapter 13
Financial Literacy of the Future: Web 3.0,
Decentralization, Defi, and Blockchain

C ongrats, you are almost at the end! We'll admit, if a lot of what
we've learned so far from this course has been new to you, you
have done amazingly! Way to take in all that knowledge—it is a lot,
but it is so important!

We've learned a lot about how our current financial systems
work, and you now have learned the best ways to "hack" it and start
building your wealth. However, the financial systems of our world
are constantly changing!

Finance has evolved so much over the past decades from going
from cash to checks, to touch pay, and SO much more! We are going
to be going over the fundamentals you need to know to be financially
literate in the years to come, as there are more and more technological
advancements in the way the world transacts money.

Introducing... *drumroll*

Financial literacy of the future! In this chapter, we will dive into
the following:

- What is Web 3.0?
- Decentralization & DeFi
- Blockchain: Understanding Cryptocurrency and How to Invest
  (Bitcoin, Ethereum, NFTs)

We know this sounds like a really flashy section… but it really is so cool!

There is so much new technology being used to transform all of the different transactions in our world — especially for those who are missing out on financial systems due to various reasons, including distrust in banks and inaccessibility to them. To fully understand how new financial technology (**FinTech**, for short!) and systems are trying to solve a lot of problems of the present, we need to first take a small step back to understand the brief history of the internet.

I. The History of the Internet + Web 3.0

History of the internet

So… you are probably wondering, what on earth does the internet have anything to do with helping you build and strengthen your financial literacy? Back then, really not much… But now, it has everything to do with it — especially if you want to keep up with the times!

When we think of the internet, it is easy to think of search engines, like Google, Yahoo, Bing, or anything else you use. However, that is not really what we mean by the internet. When we talk about the history of the internet, there are three specific stages that we need to learn about: Web 1.0, Web 2.0, and Web 3.0.

Web 3.0, Decentralization, DeFi, and Blockchain

Web 1.0: Consumption; Read-only

Web 1.0 — often pronounced as "web one" or "web one point oh" — is where it all started.[131] Web 1.0 refers to the first basic generation of the World Wide Web — yes, that is where your "www." from every URL came from!

The beginning of Web 1.0 really started around 1991. This is when there were not many content creators on the internet. Content creators were those who could afford a computer and knew how to create websites and/or contribute to them. This is very different from the present day, where literally anyone can be a content creator just by posting a Tweet or TikTok to the world! During Web 1.0, most users of the internet were not content creators, but rather content consumers. Web 1.0 was a time of content consumption and reading only. Think… blogs, forums, static pages, etc. Overall, Web 1.0 is known as a content delivery network (CDN) that allows users to showcase information on personal websites.

Web 2.0: Interaction; Read and write

Meanwhile, many understand the beginning of Web 2.0 to be in 2004 as a result of the First Web 2.0 conference.

Web 2.0 is the more advanced second generation of the internet, when websites across the world could highlight user-generated content and allow users and their content to interact with each other. Web 2.0 ushered in social media's first red carpet entrance, with the founding of platforms as early as Myspace, Facebook, MSN, or AIM,

---

131   Essex, D., Kerner, S. M., & Gillis, A. S. (2023, September 9). What is web 3.0 (WEB3)? definition, guide and history. WhatIs.com.

to more currently popular platforms like TikTok. Web 2.0 is not just limited to social media platforms, but it can also include podcasting, blogging, tagging other users, messaging, voting, and, really, anything else that allow users to interact with one another — Web 2.0 is a period of interaction, including both reading AND writing.

Technically, we are still living in a Web 2.0 world, but we are at a big transition point in establishing the beginning of the early adoption of Web 3.0.

Web 3.0: Decentralization; Read, write, and own

Web 3.0 is the third and most recent generation of the internet. This is where we'll need you to really pay attention, because we have to understand the problem of centralization in order to fully grasp why Web 3.0 exists.

II. Understanding Centralization vs. Decentralization

Centralization

In this case, "**centralization**" refers to one entity having total control over an entire platform.

Here's an example....

There is a lot of controversy around big tech companies (like the Web 2.0 platforms mentioned — X (formerly Twitter), Facebook, TikTok, etc.) having ownership over a lot of our data and personal information. Data ownership refers to having the legal rights and complete control over that information... Sound familiar? It is *centralized*.

However, this has been a super controversial topic, because data ownership often fails to protect people's privacy. This is because when data is transferred, users do not have the chance to approve or refuse their data being used. But when it does, and people do have the option, your data can also be stolen and used by hackers.

This is a problem because we are constantly creating data in every decision we make in our online presence, whether publicly on social media and forums, or more privately on how we click through our apps on our phones, reply to our emails, search things on our browsers, swipe on dating apps, and more. The scary part is that many people have a hard time processing concerns of the private side — it feels like you are always being watched.

The ironic part is, even though it is data about us, we ourselves do not actually own that data. That doesn't feel quite right, huh?! If an organization owns your data and uses it to target you for ads — and even worse, if they get hacked — your life gets impacted in some way.

The centralized nature of our data in the hands of large organizations (that are hard to keep accountable and may be susceptible to hacking) presents a problem. Web 3.0 is a solution to solve this problem.

Decentralization

What makes Web 3.0 different is **decentralization**. The opposite of centralization, decentralization means that a single entity does NOT have control over all data and processing. This means that decentralization is meant to put power and ownership back into internet users' hands. With this, **Web 3.0** is all about ownership, and various applications of Web 3.0 focus on reading, writing, and owning your own data.[132] Here is an image from Coinbase to demonstrate visually what this can look like.[133]

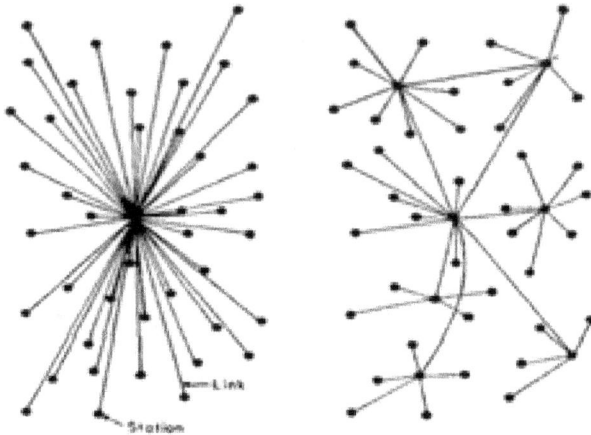

In the centralized image (left), there is a *central* point of reference.[134] For the decentralized image (right), there are many points of references, and they are not truly centralized like in the first image. So they are *decentralized*.

To understand this in application, we can look to the contexts of social media and content creation. In this scope, centralization refers to the control of data and content by a single entity, such as a major social media company. This means your data is stored on the company's servers, and they dictate how content is distributed and monetized.

On the other hand, decentralization distributes the control across a network, often using blockchain technology, which can empower

---

132   GeeksforGeeks. (2023a, July 2). Difference between web 1.0, web 2.0, and web 3.0. GeeksforGeeks.

133   Coinbase. (n.d.). A simple guide to the web3 stack. Coinbase.

134   Buterin, V. (2017, February 6). The meaning of decentralization. Medium.

users with more control over their content and data privacy. For an everyday user, decentralization could mean greater say in how personal data is used and shared, potentially reducing the reach of targeted advertising. It might also allow for more direct compensation for content creation, as intermediaries are removed.

As for content consumption, a decentralized platform could offer a wider variety of content that isn't filtered by a central algorithm. For data privacy, decentralization could mean a reduced risk of large-scale data breaches, as information is not stored in a single, centralized database. This also impacts how you might post or download photos, with potentially faster and more secure transfers due to the distributed nature of storage in decentralized systems.

For another example, the World Wide Web is NOT centralized. There is no one person who owns the entire internet. The internet is made up of all who contribute to it, so it is decentralized.

Overall, Web 3.0's decentralized nature has been actively applied to various industries, like gaming, social content, communication, and especially finance, which is where **Decentralized Finance (DeFi)** comes in!

III. DeFi

There is decentralized borrowing, decentralized lending, and lots more! Your head is probably spinning, and that is okay — ours was too when we first learned about it!

Before we get too ahead of ourselves, we need to take a bit more time to understand why DeFi is actually decentralized:

Why does DeFi exist?

As we've learned, decentralization has its perks! But how can it help in the world of finance? Let's understand the main problem DeFi solves, inspired by an article from Hackernoon.[135]

Imagine... your best friend is going away on a trip and needs you to lend him some money before he leaves. Whether or not you actually want to, let's say you agree to lend him money.

The next is to call your bank or go online to make a transaction to your friend's account. You transfer $1,000, and it shows up in your bank statement. Once it is done, you tell your friend that the $1,000 is now in his account, and he is able to use it however he pleases.

In this scenario, you and your friend trusted the bank to make the transaction on your behalf. The funny thing with online transactions is, money doesn't physically move unless you take it out in cash. In this case, it is simply the number $1,000 added onto your ledger/record from your online bank statement. This was a very centralized process that depended on the bank acting as a middleman.

You ⟶ Your Friend $1,000

The strange thing to think about is, lots of things can probably happen with a bank. What if the person you were on a call with put in $800 or $1,200, and not the requested amount of $1,000? What if the person at the bank had done this by accident, or worse, on purpose? What if an outsider hacks into the system and that amount is just gone forever, and there is nothing to prove it? With these reasons, it

---

135   WTF is the blockchain?. HackerNoon. (n.d.).

is a bit more understandable why there is a big unbanked population in the US.

There are lots of variables that could cause issues…but what if you didn't actually need the bank? This is where DeFi comes in.

Decentralized Peer-to-Peer Networks: Let's Get Down to Blockchain!

DeFi relies on the idea that we don't really need a bank to approve transactions, but rather, we can approve them in an accountable peer-to-peer way.

Let's say you have a small group of five friends, including yourself, and every one of you is given a notebook to act as a ledger.

Now, imagine Friend #1 wants to send Friend #5 a total of $20. Just like a bank does not actually move the money, you and your friends do not either. But you all acknowledge that Friend #1 wants to give Friend #5 the $20. You all approve it, and you approve it by writing that down in your ledger (a record of transactions).

Friend #1 ⟶ Friend #5 .... $20

The transactions keep happening in the same process. Let's say you have the following (below), but then you run out of space on that first piece of paper in your notebook.

Friend #1 ⟶ Friend #5 .... $20
Friend #2 ⟶ Friend #3 .... $30
Friend #2 ⟶ Friend #4 .... $60
Friend #3 ⟶ Friend #5 .... $20

You don't just simply turn the page and continue. There is a process to follow. Before we turn the page, we have to certify that this page is correct and that all friends have contributed to it, as well as confirm the validity of the written information. We certify it by creating a unique password that everyone agrees on. This password is like the lock that allows for the information to be kept safe—no hackers allowed! This whole system is built on trust and accountability through various people, not just one single entity, like the bank.

The process of creating this password is called "**mining**," and it is not really a straightforward password like "Password1234," but randomized and cryptic. Imagine you and your friends use a machine to create the password. If you want the number three to be in the password, you enter in "3" to the machine, and it tells you to use "akdew" in place of the number "3." No one knows what "akdew" means, and who knows what the translations of the numbers 4, 5, and 6 are like?! The nature of the machine you are using is meant to be completely random every time with no way to figure out its pattern.

The whole point is that you and your friends all know what numbers you added in and agreed on an encrypted, complicated password to make sure that first page you all filled out is forever safe—and in technical terms, non-fungible (a topic we'll review more in depth in Chapter 15).

You and your friends enter a few more numbers into the machine, and you have "akdewhaldkfjadfahdlfakieec." That is now the official password to seal off and protect the information you have listed on the first pages of all your notebooks. And once it is sealed, it is forever sealed; no one, not even any of you can change it.

But let's say somehow someone did change it, whether or not it was any of your friends or a mischievous hacker! You want to be able to prove that it was changed so no one loses their money wrongfully. All you or any of your friends would have to do is feed the passcode you all created back into the machine. If the machine does not say "akdewhaldkfjadfahdlfakieec," it is confirmed that something changed on the page. Also, the fact that there were five of you is very creditable — when multiple people are able to verify something, it is much more reliable as opposed to you making an argument against a single entity.

You did all this for one single page. Now you have the rest of the notebook to go through. For each page, you repeat the same process.

Okay, yes, we know that was a looooong example, but this is basically how blockchain works!

By definition, a **blockchain** is a decentralized digital ledger that records different transactions in a distributed network.

We know that definition was a whole lot of mumbo-jumbo! Let's deconstruct this a bit...

The key words of that definition we need to focus on are "ledger" and "distributed network."

A **ledger** in traditional finance and accounting is "a book or record containing accounts to which debits and credits are posted from books of original entries."[136] Basically, imagine your example notebook with all of your financial statements!

---

136   Merriam-Webster. (n.d.). Ledger definition & meaning. Merriam-Webster.

When we are adding up items in our financial statements, we are recording every transaction. **Our banks usually approve and record those transactions on our behalf.** But as we know, banks are centralized institutions and sometimes get hacked. The chance of fraudulent activity or error is a reason for why many unbanked people have strong distrust in banks!

Whether or not you have a bank account, the centralized nature of banks is sometimes a concern for individuals.[137] But if you decentralize your ledger and how your transactions are recorded, that can have a massive impact on what banking means, ultimately building greater trust and inclusion.[138] That is exactly what happened when you and your four other friends created a process together and kept each other accountable, creating a cryptic method of verifying each page of that notebook.

In the world of blockchain, ledgers are decentralized because of the help of **nodes**. Nodes are hardware or people that co-write, approve, and encode the data that gets put into the ledger, and overall, into the blockchain. So, in this example, you and your friends, and even the mysterious machine, are the nodes! The entire approval and encoding process is called "**mining**" — not by tunneling into the earth to mine for gold, but think of mining in the sense of extracting something valuable! Every time you co-sealed off a page together with your peers with a complicated password, you were mining. And the password and seal itself is the equivalent of a "**smart contract.**"

---

137   Cointelegraph. (n.d.). Banking the unbanked: How defi can help the low-income population. Cointelegraph.

138   Maksimenka, I. (2021, January 31). Defi is the future of banking that humanity deserves. Cointelegraph.

Also, in the example, you and your friends hand a notebook full of various pages. And we only mentioned what went on the first page. Think of each page as a "block." When we add up all the pages to each other, they are linked and "chained" together — hence the name blockchain!

In essence, blockchain represents a fairly revolutionary concept, enabling an accountable, peer-to-peer (decentralized) way of co-writing and co-encrypting (mining) various pieces of data (blocks) with the help of people/hardware (nodes), which create intense, hard-to-solve chunks of code/passwords (smart contracts), to go into a larger group of information (chain).

After understanding the concept of blocks linked together as a 'blockchain', it's important to recognize the role of distributed networks in this system. In a distributed network, the blockchain doesn't reside in one central location but is copied and stored across a network of computers, known as nodes. Each node has a full copy of the blockchain, making the information on the blockchain transparent and immutable. This distribution ensures that no single entity has control over the entire chain and that the information is publicly accessible, enhancing security and trust. Any changes to one block would require a consensus across the network, making unauthorized alterations almost impossible. This decentralized nature is what makes blockchain a powerful tool for secure, transparent transactions without the need for a trusted central authority.

The integration of blockchain into distributed networks is just the tip of the iceberg in the broader context of Web 3.0 and cryptography. We're just starting to see the changes that Web 3.0 and new security technology will bring to our online lives. This new wave of the internet is all about giving power back to us, the users, allowing us to control our information and how we share it with others. With better security built into the very fabric of the internet, we'll be able to talk, share, and shop with more confidence that our data is safe. What we're seeing now is only the beginning, and we can look forward to even more amazing changes that will make our online world better and safer.

IV. Cheat Code Recap

1. Web 1.0 was a time of content consumption and reading only. Web 2.0 is a period of interaction, including both reading AND writing. Web 3.0 is the third and most recent generation of the internet, where decentralization allows users to read, write, and own content.

2. Centralization refers to the idea of an entity having total control over an entire platform; decentralization means that a single entity does not have control over all data and processing.

3. Decentralized Finance (DeFi) refers to financial services and applications built on blockchain technology, often removing intermediaries.

4. Blockchain is a decentralized digital ledger that records different transactions in a distributed network.

Chapter 14
Financial Literacy of the Future: Making Sense of Cryptocurrency

Blockchain is part of **Layer 0**, or the **settlement layer**, which is the most foundational layer that defines DeFi, how it works, and why it exists.[139] So basically, without blockchain — which makes decentralization possible — and this overall settlement layer, it would be impossible for DeFi to exist.

You are probably feeling a bit overwhelmed about the fact that we had an entire section on blockchain, and it isn't even Layer 1 yet! Not to worry, we won't need to understand all other layers too in depth, but it is important to know the differences between each one as we begin to relate everything you've learned about financial literacy to the trends of today.

Below, we've listed all layers of DeFi (as well as Web 3.0 as a whole). Because DeFi and Web 3.0 are still so new and nascent concepts, some sources might have different names for each layer listed; but regardless, each layer still performs the same function regardless of the newly coined names. We will continue to go in depth into Layers 1 and 2 for the remainder of the course, since they will be the most relevant to the theme of financial literacy.

- Layer 0: Settlement Layer

---

139   Binance Academy. (2023, July 4). What is layer 0 in Blockchain?

- Layer 1: Protocol Layer
- Layer 2: Asset Layer
- Layer 3: Application Layer
- Layer 4: Aggregation Layer

I. Foundations of Cryptocurrency

Next up, we have **Layer 1,** also known as the **protocol layer**! When we think of the word protocol, the first thing that might come to mind is a type of system to follow to help smoothly govern and go about a specific situation.

The protocol layer does exactly this. It is essentially the layer that needs to translate the many blockchain codes from the settlement layer so that they can actually have some type of use in the real world, besides just being chunks of crazy encrypted code!

The best and arguably first pioneering example of protocol is Bitcoin! (YES, you will finally learn what Bitcoin is!!)

Bitcoin

Bitcoin is one of the first popularized decentralized digital currencies that could actually be transferred on a peer-to-peer network.[140] Bitcoin was launched in 2009 through a paper published by the mysterious pseudonym Santoshi Nakamoto.[141] This paper proposed that Bitcoin has the potential to operate as an online currency that

---

140   Reiff, N. (n.d.). Bitcoin vs. Ethereum: What's the difference?

141   Nakamoto, S. (2008). Bitcoin: A peer-to-peer electronic cash system. Decentralized business review.

does not require any type of central authority (basically, a bank). This paper explained all sorts of different natures of Bitcoin and the entire concept of blockchain.

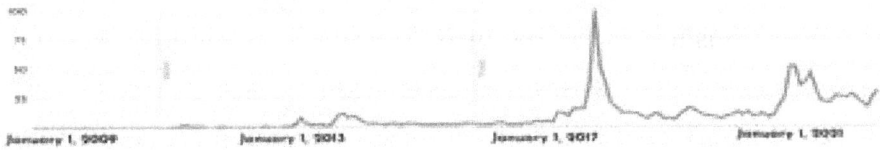

This chart is sourced from Google Trends, featuring Bitcoin's popularity in its search engine. Its peak popularity was in January 2018.

Though similar, Bitcoin is not a stock, even though you can invest in it. It is a Web 3.0, decentralized type of asset, known as cryptocurrency.

Just for further clarification, cryptocurrency (often called "crypto" for short) is a digital currency in which transactions are recorded and put into action with the help of a decentralized system, known as cryptography. Cryptography and this decentralized system are fancy terms for the entire mumbo-jumbo process with nodes, smart contracts, etc. that makes the blockchain encryption process possible—it is basically the process that takes place in that crazy "machine" we feed numbers into and spits out code. A way we can think of cryptography and cryptocurrency to help us remember what it stands for is the word "cryptic," which is a word that refers to anything mysterious, obscure, or hard to determine.

Further, because Bitcoin operates like a decentralized public stock, the value of Bitcoin is determined through a decentralized system rather than a centralized authority. It is a very "next level" stock. However, the major caveat is that it is not very fast; it takes a while for transactions to process because the entire system of blockchain it runs on can only process seven transactions per second. Yes, we know one second isn't much time (especially if it needs to be mined!), so seven transactions per second might seem like a lot. But if *everyone* in the world wanted to invest in Bitcoin, this could be painfully slow.

Bitcoin, however, is not the only cryptocurrency. It is also not the first one, but it is the first one that received popular attention. There are SO many types out there!

Ethereum and Ether (Layers 1 and 2)

Another talked-about cryptocurrency is Ether (ETH) — pronounced "ee-thur." It is the second-largest cryptocurrency by market value, so it is worth a lot![142] It was launched in 2015 as a byproduct of Ethereum (yes, Ether and Ethereum are not *exactly* the same thing).

Ethereum is arguably the largest and best-established decentralized software platform that specializes in enabling the use of smart contracts and decentralized applications (dApps — think of your Web 2.0 apps in the App Store but they operate on some form of decentralization or blockchain, so they are a lot more secure). Ethereum is basically the thing that allows smart coders and developers to build and launch

---

142   Frankenfield, J. (n.d.). What is ethereum and how does it work?. Investopedia.

more decentralized products and applications. On top of this, it can also process close to two times the transactions that Bitcoin can handle per second.

When Ethereum first launched, it also released Ether (ETH). The interesting thing is that being a cryptocurrency was not what it was intended to be made for. Ether is also used to run different blockchain applications on the Ethereum network. You can think of Ether as the fuel that makes it possible for Ethereum to function.

Ether and Bitcoin are similar in a variety of ways, including the following:

- They are both digital cryptocurrencies
- They are both decentralized (they are not regulated by a central authority)
- They make use of blockchain technology

However, they were created for different purposes:

- Bitcoin: Created as an alternative to a national currency that does not rely on a centralized authority
- Ether: Created NOT to be a currency (although it is one) but to be the "fuel" to make Ethereum function for its role with smart contracts and dApps.

However, Ethereum (the platform) is considered Layer 1, and Ether (the cryptocurrency) is considered Layer 2.

Layer 2 solutions are systems that are built on top of underlying blockchain architecture. Bitcoin is not considered Layer 2, but rather Layer 1. This is because it does not have a platform to go off of. Ether, however, has Ethereum to leverage as a foundational network layer. To distinguish them to be even more clear, some Web 3.0/crypto community members call Ether (the cryptocurrency) "Ethereum layer 2" and Ethereum (the platform) "Ethereum layer 1."

II. Case Study: DOGE to the moon!

Bitcoin and Ether are huge in the world of cryptocurrency. But they are not alone! Over these past years, Dogecoin really made a HUGE red-carpet entrance as well!

Quite frankly, Dogecoin is known as the joker of cryptocurrency. It was inspired by the Doge meme, based on a 2010 photograph of a Shiba Inu dog named Kabosu, which is overlaid by Comic Sans text written in broken English.[143] The Doge meme became the top-ranked meme in 2013 on Know Your Meme!

---

143   Leech, O. (2021, September 14). How dogecoin became so popular. CoinDesk Latest Headlines RSS.

In that same year, Adobe Marketing Manager Jackson Palmer and software engineer Billy Markus set out to create a cryptocurrency, known as **Dogecoin**, out of this meme to make it "as ridiculous as possible."

Dogecoin's design was meant to reflect the meme itself in its random nature. The ironic part is that it was inspired by another cryptocurrency called Luckycoin—which was inspired by Litecoin and Bitcoin.[144] Luckycoin had a system to randomly award its miners. Sometimes miners would receive nothing, and sometimes they would receive several thousands of free coins for writing up new contracts to create new blocks.

Yes, we know this sounds silly, but as we mentioned, the entire creation of Dogecoin was meant to be a joke. The creators Palmer and Markus actually made sure it was designed this way in hopes that its randomness would annoy miners of Dogecoin so much that they would not feel compelled to actually use the token as a payment method. However, the complete opposite happened. It turns out that the outrageousness of its design was a lighthearted and accessible way for aspiring miners to get some experience with cryptocurrency.

After only one month after Dogecoin launched, the official Dogecoin website earned over 1 million views and went viral! There was even a Reddit channel, r/Dogecoin, which accumulated over 19,000 users, and Dogecoin's price went up by 300%! But unfortunately, later that year, Dogecoin hit a big bump in the road. It got hacked for the first time by someone who stole 11 million Dogecoin (approximately

---

144   Napoletano, E. (2023, September 22). What is Litecoin? how does it work?. Forbes. https://www.forbes.com/advisor/investing/cryptocurrency/litecoin/

$12,000 in value at the time). This became known as the "Dogecoin Christmas hack."

Over the past few years, it's been trying to pick up momentum. In 2018, Elon Musk, founder and CEO of Tesla, began to interact with Dogecoin in a very interesting way. There were Twitter scam bots that were impersonating Elon Musk to try to steal other Twitter users' cryptocurrency! How crazy is that!!

With this, Musk reached out to Dogecoin co-founder Jackson Palmer to help. After successful execution, Musk tweeted "Doge might be my fav cryptocurrency. It's pretty cool." as a response to winning an April Fool's Day poll to become Dogecoin's newly elected CEO.

I am Hodler 🔑 @iamhodler · Apr 2, 2019
@elonmusk You can't decline!

> **Dogecoin** @dogecoin · 16h
> We have listened to your concerns. We have decided that Dogecoin does need a CEO. Someone who can lead us into the future while maintaining the core values of what we are.
>
> Below are the candidates, vote wisely.
>
> @VitalikButerin @SatoshiLite @elonmusk @MarshallHayner
>
> | Vitalik Buterin | 9% |
> | Charlie Lee | 8% |
> | Elon Musk ⊘ | 49% |
> | Marshall Hayner | 33% |
>
> 3,581 votes · 7 hours 32 minutes left

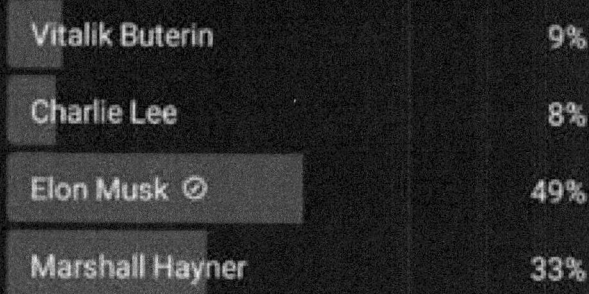

Elon Musk ✓
@elonmusk · Follow

Dogecoin might be my fav cryptocurrency. It's pretty cool.

5:24 AM · Apr 2, 2019

Elon Musk ✅
10.7K Tweets

Elon Musk ✅
@elonmusk

🛸 🛩 ☀ 🚗 🌐 ⬭, meme necromancer, former CEO Dogecoin

📅 Joined June 2009

83 Following   **33.3M** Followers

Elon riding the wave

Prior to this, Elon Musk posted various tweets mentioning that Tesla could only be bought using Bitcoin. But at this point in time, Elon Musk, the wealthiest person in the world (as of 2022), is now supporting Dogecoin!

Musk has been continuing to tweet occasionally about Dogecoin's value over the past few years, and whenever he has, the value would go up a substantial amount (anywhere from 25% to 800% growth!) just moments after he had tweeted about it. Can you imagine one person making the value of a cryptocurrency worth $0.001 to be as much as $0.45?! Talk about a strong influencer marketing game!!

In all seriousness, social media outlets like X (formerly Twitter), Reddit, and Discord are truly game-changing platform to affect market trends! This was how the market value of GameStop skyrocketed in 2021 as well!

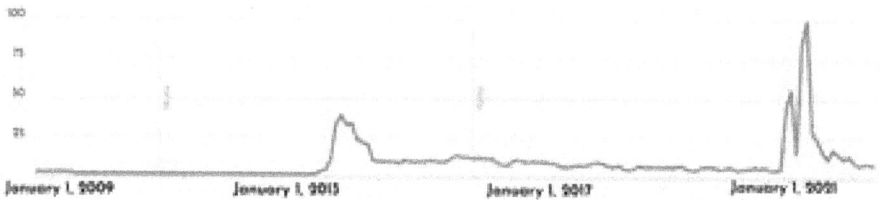

This chart is sourced from Google Trends, featuring "Doge's" popularity in its search engine. Its peak popularity was in May 2021.

Below, we have included some snapshots of Elon Musk's tweets about Dogecoin:

Elon Musk ✓
@elonmusk · Follow

Ball, Frisbee, or **Stick?**
The ultimate guide to the perfect game of catch

how to get the best treats

PLAYING FETCH WITH

CINZA
WHIPPET

The Goodest *Issue*

5:47 PM · Jan 28, 2021

Elon Musk
@elonmusk · Follow

It's inevitable

dogecoin
standard

global
financial system

8:58 PM · Jul 17, 2020

Read the full conversation on Twitter

Elon Musk ✓
@elonmusk · Follow

The future currency of Earth

Dogecoin to the Moooonn	71.3%
All other crypto combined	28.7%

2,432,725 votes · Final results

11:51 PM · Feb 5, 2021

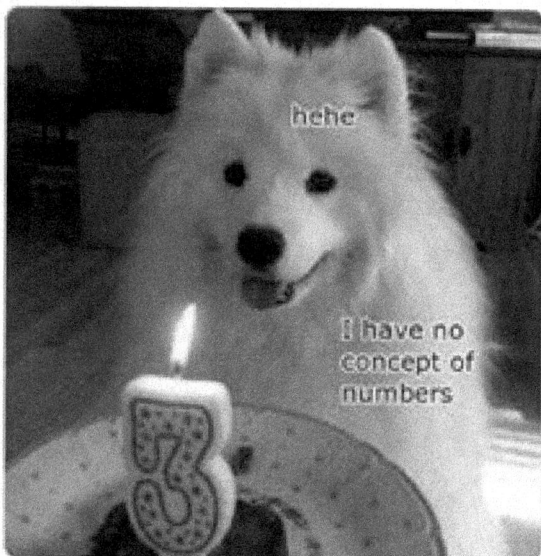

Elon Musk @
@elonmusk

Doge Barking at the Moon

12:33 AM · Apr 15, 2021 · Twitter for iPhone

46.8K Retweets **5,208** Quote Tweets **320K** Likes

III. How to think about investing in cryptocurrency

So... obviously, there are LOTS of different types of cryptocurrencies out there. If something like Dogecoin could get as popular as it did, the possibilities really are ENDLESS! But how do you even decide on how to invest in them?

Solana and the Blockchain Tri-lemma

Solana: Speed & Fees

Solana is another type of cryptocurrency, and one of the more popular ones since it was founded more recently in 2020. The biggest things that stand out about Solana are its transaction speed and its affordable fees.

We mentioned earlier that Bitcoin's transaction speed is seven transactions per second, and Ether's speed is about two times faster... but Solana comes in at a whopping 50,000 transactions per second!! That is over 7,142 times faster than Bitcoin.

With this, Solana sounds like a no-brainer to invest in. It is not really because of how many transactions take place per second, but rather the effect of that: it is about how quickly the transactions in the market are settled and confirmed. This means that if the transaction speed and time are faster, you are able to receive more live-time updates about its real time market value, and your transaction will also be more accurately up-to-date if you choose to buy or sell it.

The second advantage is that Solana does not have fees. Yes, this means that Bitcoin, Ether, and literally every other cryptocurrency out there has additional fees you need to pay.

Why is this? It is simply because mining is not a cheap process! Ethereum miners are compensated for their work in deploying smart contracts (verifying transactions and securing the network). This is called a **gas fee.**

Cryptocurrencies have gotten backlash from the public about not being sustainable financial solutions and that they actually waste a lot of energy and have a big carbon footprint.[145] However, when gas fees are lower, that simply means less energy is expended, in turn reducing carbon footprint. Ironically, gas fees are not related in any way to actual gasoline prices or environmental impact.

The neat thing about Solana is that its transaction fee is as low as $0.01, while Bitcoin and Ether are notorious for high gas fees!

However, Solana is not perfect, either — which is why we are using it for this example to help you understand the Blockchain Tri-lemma.

The Blockchain Tri-Lemma

The Blockchain Tri-lemma is a framework you can use to analyze different types of cryptocurrencies and how you should think about their viability for investment.[146] The Blockchain Tri-lemma essentially suggests that there is a three-way tradeoff that happens between

---

145   Fontao, A. (2021, November 3). Environmental impacts of cryptocurrency: A different kind of "mining." The Daily Californian

146   Musharraf, M. (2023, July 22). What is the blockchain trilemma?. Ledger. https://www.ledger.com/academy/what-is-the-blockchain-trilemma

scalability, security, and decentralization. The following bullets below defines these three concepts a bit more in depth:

- **Scalability**: How fast can it be to complete transactions?
  - » Throughput: The transaction speed
- **Security**: How safe and secure is it? How likely will someone be able to hack into it and steal cryptocurrency like the Dogecoin Christmas hack?
- **Decentralization**: How decentralized is it? Is it to any degree governed by a centralized authority?

Overall, there are huge debates about Solana because it has scalability (50,000 transactions per second is a LOT!); however, its speed has been scrutinized because many believe that it makes compromises on its security and decentralization.

On the other hand, Ether Layer 2 allows for an application to have scalability because it offloads its transaction to the Ethereum network (AKA Ethereum Layer 1). As it does this, Ether is able to maintain its decentralization aspects to be usable and uphold its integrity to its users.

Overall within the crypto community, huge debates have been rampant about the Blockchain Tri-lemma, so make sure to do your due diligence when you debate on how you might want to invest in cryptocurrency!

Investing and Paying in Crypto

Since it was first introduced, Bitcoin has been making some headway in being accepted as a currency that can be used for payment in stores and in our financial systems. The same is being done for other types of crypto, as well.

Regardless of whether you decide to invest in cryptocurrencies now or later, some commonly used crypto brokerage platforms include:

- Coinbase
- Voyager
- BlockFi
- Uphold
- Kraken
- eToro
- Bitcoin IRA
- Crypto.com
- Binance
- Hodlnaut

Many say that the best way to truly understand crypto is to start investing, so now is the time to start little by little!

IV. Cheat Code Recap

1. The concept of cryptocurrency is separated into different "layers" to help it operate.
2. Bitcoin is one of the first popularized decentralized digital currencies that can be transferred on a peer-to-peer network.

3. The Blockchain Tri-lemma, essentially suggests that there is a three-way tradeoff that happens between scalability, security, and decentralization.

Chapter 15
*Financial Literacy of the Future: Building
(More) Wealth in a Web 3.0 World*

A lrighty! We are at the final stretch of our financial literacy journey! You've made it—just one more bit to go!

In this last section, we're going to bring it back full circle to the entire concept of building wealth, but in a Web 3.0 world. Just understanding the concept of blockchain and cryptocurrency are the foundation of what we will go over here. One part of building wealth is investing, and though extremely risky, cryptocurrency is an option to invest in and follow. Here, we will also be going over more ways to grow your Web 3.0 assets and navigate opportunities in a virtual Web 3.0 world.

I. Tokenizing assets

What is tokenization?
Ethereum has received a lot of attention these past few years because there is so much potential in using it. Tokenization plays a big role within the world of Web 3.0 and Ethereum. Tokenization is the act of converting the value of something into blockchain terms to

give you ownership in the Web 3.0 world. It is applied especially to anything that has been built on Ethereum.

In an easier way to understand tokenization, before there were subway, bus, trolley cards, or Apple/Android Pay, cities often used tokens for public transportation. You had to pay money to receive a token. The same system works at your local arcade or Chuck-E-Cheese, but also for Web 3.0! Tokens are basically substitutes for actual money, so they are hard to exploit.

Tokenizing Digital Assets

There are three categories of digital assets that can be tokenized (recall what you learned in the section on assets!)

Intangible Assets

As we mentioned, intangible assets lack a physical presence and cannot be touched. Some examples we mentioned earlier in this course include the following:

Goodwill (remember, not the store! We mean actual goodwill, which is the overall value to a company or things that cannot really be quantified)

- Brand equity
- Intellectual property (trade secrets, patents, and copyrights)
- Licensing
- Customer lists
- R&D

Fungible Assets

When something is "**fungible**" it is usually referring to its ability as an asset to be exchanged for another of similar value. With this, **fungible assets** are assets that can be replaceable by a similar type of item, which is easier to divide.

For example, the value of $20 is fungible—$20 still has the same value if it is paid in a $20 bill, two $10 bills, or twenty $1 bills. $20 in any form is fungible because any form you pay it in is still equal to the same value. Another example is how one ounce of gold is equal to another ounce of gold, or how one gallon of gas is equal to one gallon of gas. Bitcoin is fungible, too, because one Bitcoin is equal to another bitcoin.

Non-Fungible Assets

Non-fungible assets are the opposite of fungible assets. According to Investopedia, a good example is if you lend your friend your car and she returns a different car to you, despite the fact that it is the same model and type of car. Cars are not fungible with respect to ownership, but the gasoline that powers the cars is fungible. Meanwhile, other assets like diamonds (which can have different cuts, colors and sizes), homes (which, even if they were all the same home with the same design on the same street, could have different views or levels of traffic and noise), or Pokémon cards (which could have different rarities) are all non-fungible because each asset has unique qualities that can either add or deduct value.

NFTs

This type of asset might sound more familiar because of the hype around **non-fungible tokens (NFTs)** in 2021. It is built on Ethereum Layer 1, and it is a type of non-fungible asset. An NFT is a one-of-a-kind digital content, like a drawing, song tune, GIF, meme, etc. The biggest thing to know about NFTs is that it's been known for its "collectible" aspect, like artwork.[147] So, think of there being only ONE digital copy of the Mona Lisa. Because it is built on blockchain (particularly, Ethereum, which is considered to be more robust in terms of decentralization and scalability), it means the ownership is protected, so the original can't be changed or copied—so you can't copy the Mona Lisa or copy the Declaration of Independence like they did in National Treasure (sorry, Nicholas Cage!). Nevertheless, though the original can't be copied on the blockchain, like everything on the internet, you can see the same memes, pictures, songs, and videos on so many different media platforms—but there will always be only one original.

NFTs are a very controversial topic—some people believe they will be the future, while others believe they are a total sham. It depends on whether you're the artist/creator or the buyer/collector. Artists get the chance to sell their work and get paid every time their NFT is sold, while buyers/collectors have the pride of saying they own the NFT. The most controversial part of NFTs revolves around its cost. Various people will pay hundreds of thousands of dollars for an NFT.

---

147   Abrol, A. (2023, September 27). Web 3.0 vs. metaverse: A detailed comparison [updated]. Blockchain Council.

Imagine paying that much for a Pokémon trading card. Think of it as fine art collecting — it is for some people, and not so much for others.

The Bored Ape Yacht Club was known as the most famous NFT collection in 2020 on OpenSea — one of the largest NFT marketplaces to purchase them. Celebrities ranging from Justin Bieber, Post Malone, Kevin Hart, Jimmy Fallon, Paris Hilton, and more all own some version of this collection of art. Each of these below were sold for the following prices:

Bored Ape Yacht Club #1837: $1,575,561

Bored Ape Yacht Club #8585: $2,702,462

Bored Ape Yacht Club #8817: $3,408,000

On the other hand, another one of the most popular NFTs was created by 12-year-old Benyamin Ahmed, which he called the "Weird Whales" collection. By the end of 2021, he earned over $400,000. Probably a lot more than you would make at a lemonade stand at that age!

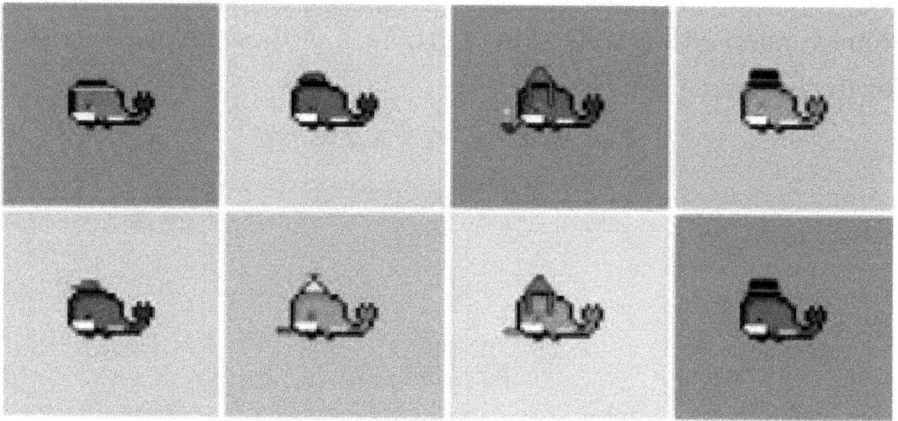

What are your thoughts about NFTs? Do you believe NFTs have a future in helping us build wealth? Why and why not?

II. Ethereum and Metaverse

Going back to our conversation about tokenization and the seemingly endless application of Ethereum, when something is tokenized, ownership is established because of tokenization's ability to, in theory, allow for us to truly gain ownership over an asset.

Outside of the examples provided, Ethereum has also gained momentum in other areas, like gaming and virtual reality. Decentraland is one of the leading virtual worlds that uses the

Ethereum blockchain to secure items contained within the world. Everything from the avatars, tokens, rewards, items, and land are all tokenized.

Decentraland is one of the leading examples of the metaverse.

Metaverse and the Race Against Big Tech

Facebook and Meta vs. Decentralization

So, your mind might suddenly be wandering off to remember Facebook's founder Mark Zuckerberg's announcement to create their own metaverse called Meta.

Just a quick clarification: metaverse is a concept that has long existed before Facebook and Meta. "**Metaverse**" is a shorthand term for virtual worlds where users can interact with each other and engage with applications and services in an extremely immersive way.[148] With this, the metaverse isn't a single game or virtual reality experience. It is an entire experience where virtual reality has real life implications—like how smart phones were able to provide us.

The term "metaverse" made its first red carpet appearance in Neal Stephenson's science fiction novel, Snow Crash, which described a virtual world. Since then, this concept has taken on a life of its own in more mainstream science fiction productions like Ready Player One, The Matrix, and shows like Black Mirror.

Facebook identified the huge opportunity in cryptocurrency but had no actual way to tap into it, and that is one of the biggest contributors for why they considered launching Meta.

---

148   Clark, M. (2021, March 3). NFTs, explained. The Verge.

The plan for the metaverse — we mean the entire metaverse as a whole, not just the company, Meta — is to use cryptocurrency as the staple currency. However, there is not just one type of metaverse. Many companies and individuals are racing to create metaverses and different opportunities within each metaverse based on different types of cryptocurrencies. With this, each metaverse has its own cryptocurrency — almost like different countries have their own currencies!

In our unit on banks earlier on, we mentioned how one of banks' functions is to help with currency exchange. The metaverse is still so new that the policies and structures around cryptocurrency exchange are non-existent!

While it is exciting to think about all the possibilities of different types of cryptocurrencies, Facebook's pivot to work on a metaverse really rubbed the crypto community the wrong way:

- **Pre-existing centralization:** The whole reason Web 3.0 has been a hot topic is because many people are tired of centralization, where one entity has absolute control. With Facebook being as big as it is, this posed a huge issue.

- **Future cryptocurrency centralization:** Beyond already being such a centralized Web 2.0 platform, Facebook/Meta also created their own cryptocurrency called **Libra**. Yes, already! Initially, Facebook considered using Bitcoin; however, the problem with Bitcoin is that seven transactions per second was too slow for what they were hoping for, and they knew Meta would not be able to leverage it sustainably. Libra can handle several thousand transactions per second, which is much faster!

However, this is a tradeoff (recall the Blockchain Tri-lemma!) because of the potential compromise in decentralization.

As a result, Facebook/Meta acknowledged this, so they set out to create their own new decentralized network across other big companies, so that all the companies could keep each other accountable and build public trust—they basically replicated the peer-to-peer distributed network at the business-wide level! Some of these companies include PayPal, Visa, Mastercard, Uber, eBay, Lyft, Stripe, Coinbase, Kiva, Spotify, and more. Each one of them contributed close to $10 million.

In theory, this could work. However, one thing users have had a hard time accepting is that users cannot see all historical transactions but only the final ledgers. This is an issue because that means users have to trust centralized authority once again to make sure everything is valid.

What are your thoughts around Facebook's/Meta's steps taken to put forth their own Libra cryptocurrency? Do you think it will succeed or fail?

Regardless, as we have learned through the Blockchain Tri-lemma, having a throughput (transaction speed) is not enough to stay competitive. It turns out that our federal government has been in conversation with Facebook/Meta and investigating Libra, and they are even worried that Libra could overthrow the entire monetary system of the US!

Because there was so much concern around this, the project was shut down as it posed too much risk. While this all happened, there was (and still is an ongoing) backlash against a centralized metaverse, which has caused people to fund different initiatives to try to overthrow Facebook/Meta's metaverse.

There are various metaverses, including some of the following:

- HyperVerse
- Decentraland
- The Sandbox
- Somnium Space
- Nakamoto
- Roblox
- Epic Games
- Bloktopia
- Cryptovoxels
- Axie Infinity
- Enijin
- Shiba Inu's Shiberse

Within each one of these, there are various companies and individuals finding various ways to get engaged and innovate new things to offer to users.

For instance, many believe NFTs have a huge presence in a "**virtual marketplace**," which will be essentially virtual reality trading grounds.[149] Many are imagining that these virtual marketplaces will

---

149   Fonarov, O. (2022, October 12). Council post: What is the role of nfts in the metaverse?. Forbes.

likely be leveraging existing social VR platforms like VRChat in the long term. With this, sellers can easily provide links and previews online to mine and "mint" digital assets in the VR space. Nike has already gotten into this as well with its own virtual "Nikeland," which has acquired a studio for making NFTs of their own products.

Other use cases include creating **art galleries** for NFTs. This is slightly different from virtual marketplaces because you can't negotiate prices in art galleries. There are museums on metaverse that are placing NFT artworks for sale, like in Cryptovoxels, which hosts art from the San Francisco Museum of Modern Art and the FC Francisco Carolinium Linz in Austria.

JP Morgan Chase is even hopping in on the opportunity and established their own bank in Decentraland in their "Metajuku Mall."

Real Estate in Web 3.0

The Lay of the Digital Land

Beyond the applications of cryptocurrency and NFTs in the metaverse, there are also opportunities to invest in virtual real estate!

We know, real life real estate is already so lucrative and so much to handle!! But the interesting thing about this is that real estate in the metaverse refers to plots of digital land that can be sold as NFTs. Various metaverses, particularly The Sandbox, have already begun taking advantage of this opportunity, as shown in the image below.

Republic Realm, a digital real estate investing firm — YES, there are digital real estate investing firms!! — metaverse land sales that took place throughout 2021. Republic Realm's report covered metaverse land sales that took place throughout 2021. Facebook's announcement to rebrand to Meta took place in October, which is no surprise as to why November's purchases of digital real estate totally skyrocketed, going from $19.5 million to $187 million of total sales!

According to Influencer Marketing Hub, The Sandbox earned a total of $350 million in sales for all of 2021 for their real estate.[150] This is a total of 65,000 transactions! Meanwhile, Decentraland came in second, earning a total of $110 million in sales with a total of 21,000 transactions! Overall, there was a total of $500 million spent in the market of virtual real estate in 2021.

Virtual real estate in the metaverse is picking up lots of momentum, but we need to remember that real estate is a very conservative industry, and buying property is challenging — especially if you have not built any wealth yet. But because of this, younger generations are entering this space and exploring their virtual real estate options and tokenizing them to grow their wealth.[151]

How to Think About Investing in Virtual Real Estate

Investing in virtual real estate is very similar to real-life real estate. But a recommended way to think about investing in virtual real estate is to relate it to a game of Monopoly (YES, another Monopoly game reference!).

The goal of the game is to buy as much property as you can, and just like Monopoly, the location of your plot of land is important —

---

150   Mileva, G. (2022, May 4). The Ultimate Guide to Metaverse Virtual Real Estate. Influencer Marketing Hub. https://influencermarketinghub.com/metaverse-virtual-real-estate/

151   YouTube. (2021). Get Ready for the 2022 Metaverse Real Estate Boom. YouTube.

you've probably noticed that the properties in Monopoly get more expensive the farther away you go from passing "Go." Areas that attract more user traffic in the metaverse are predicted to be higher in value.

Snoop Dogg, for instance, owns a digital mansion in The Sandbox metaverse, which attracts a lot of user traffic, and that means those who live around him in the metaverse will also have high-valued virtual real estate. In fact, his neighbor bought some digital land for $450,000 (which is about 71,000 SAND in The Sandbox metaverse's currency)!

While virtual real estate has been getting lots of attention, it is such a new and upcoming space that people are still trying to better understand. There are lots of things you can do with your land, like renting it out to brands or firms that need work space in the metaverse, but the biggest hesitations revolve around the fact that the metaverse runs on cryptocurrency. Cryptocurrency's value tends to fluctuate, so it can be a risky investment.

Whether or not you think investing in virtual real estate is for you, we hope this was helpful in helping you better understand what it's all about! If it is something of interest to you, here are the recommended steps you can take to invest, sourced from an article by Influencer Marketing Hub:[152]

1. **Decide which metaverse you want to join:** As we mentioned, there are lots of options, but the most popular ones as of 2021 are The Sandbox and Decentraland.

---

152   Mileva, G. (2022a, May 4). How to invest in Virtual Real Estate (Metaverse Real Estate Guide). Influencer Marketing Hub /

2. **Set up a digital wallet:** Do this after deciding which metaverse you want to join because every single one has a different type of cryptocurrency!

3. **Browse the NFT marketplace:** Every property in a metaverse is an NFT! Crazy to think, right? With this, like all NFTs and investment opportunities, you need to figure out your investment strategy. Will you be selling the land after it reaches a certain value? Do you plan to rent it out? Who do you plan to rent it out to? Will someone else inherit it? Yes, we know, it goes super in depth!

4. **Link your wallet to the platform's marketplace:** This works in a similar way of connecting your credit/debit card to a platform.

5. **Invest!**

Would you want to invest in virtual real estate? Why or why not?

Pros and cons of the metaverse

Obviously, there are lots of up-and-coming opportunities happening in the metaverse! But what are your thoughts on it? The general public has outlined various of pros and cons to the metaverse in early online forums, and some of the more commonly mentioned considerations include the following:

Pros:

- A more engaging and immersive way to connect with others. It can also be less awkward.
- A new and refreshing way to work from home.

- A new way to grow brand loyalty and media presence.
- It can redefine how we think about education. Imagine going on a virtual field trip to a different country, or to Paleolithic times!
- A new way to build wealth.
- It presents opportunities for businesses.
- It can have a positive impact on cryptocurrencies and NFTs.
- You can travel the world without leaving your home.
- It can help us all gain new technological skill sets and create new types of job opportunities.
- You can meet your loved ones whenever you'd like to.

Cons:
- It is a lot to even learn and understand what it is.
- The technology is expensive and presents inequity issues (e.g. Facebook's Oculus and Microsoft's Hololens are expensive).
- High energy consumption (remember, this is related to gas fees!)
- Feeling a little Black Mirror-ish or like the Matrix: What is reality?
- Is it really safe and secure? Particularly, is it safe for our children?
- There can be a negative impact on our culture as a whole and even mental health issues.
- There are laws that need to be defined in metaverse.
- How will it impact our sense of compassion?

- There is worry over how we will interact with the real world post-full adoption of metaverse.

What are your overall thoughts on the promise of the metaverse? Which reasons listed are most valid to you personally? Which are more questionable? What are the advantages and disadvantages that you personally see outside of the pros and cons listed?

III. Navigating Web 3.0 in today's economy

You might either feel exhilarated or really apprehensive about the metaverse, NFTs, crypto, and everything that Web 3.0 is presenting to our world.

It is important to acknowledge that it is still SO new, and we as a society are still trying to learn a lot more about it and its possibilities, as well as the risks.

The fact is, we are also living in a fairly turbulent economy. Building wealth is already so much to think about in a Web 2.0 world. We hope that you will leverage all that we have guided you through to build your wealth in every way possible so that you can live the life you want, whether it's in the physical or virtual space!

As you think about how to invest today and in the future, learning about past critical financial events will be informative to your journey in building wealth in a Web 3.0 World!

The **Dot-Com Boom and Bust** can tell us a lot about what is happening with our economy now.[153] Back in 2000, lots of companies

---

153   Brown, J. (2021, December 10). The secret to investing in 2021? look to the 2000 dot-com bubble. Forbes.

were getting crazy amounts of funding to pursue exciting new opportunities in the Web 2.0 world (remember, at that time, it was in the same stage that Web 3.0 is for us now!) but were providing little value to people.

Before that bubble burst, investors funded major infrastructure projects that required laying fiber optic cables in the ground and in buildings so that computers could be connected to the internet to propel the age of Web 2.0 forward. This was super expensive, and when the bubble burst, all that funding that poured into laying wires into the ground seemed like a lost cause. There was so much uncertainty, similar to how there is now. However, without that happening, there are debates on how the internet industry may have evolved much more slowly than it did.

When recession hit, many lost their jobs and many companies had shut down, but those who were able to sustain themselves kept building. In 2002, when the market had hit an all-time low, Mark Zuckerberg officially published the first version of Facebook!

All this to say, even though the economy is in a turbulent state now, there is opportunity in being open-minded to learn more about the potential of Web 3.0 and really leverage it to build your own wealth.

IV. Cheat Code Recap

1. Tokenization is the act of converting the value of something into blockchain terms to give you ownership in the Web 3.0 world.

2. Fungible assets are assets that can be replaceable by a similar type of item, which is easier to divide; non-fungible assets are not replaceable.

3. Metaverse is perceived to present potential up-and-coming opportunities for growing wealth.

4. The Dot-Com Boom and Bust can tell us a lot about what is happening with our economy now.

CONCLUSION

Your financial journey is just starting, and it's a lifelong one. Embrace the learning, adapt to changing financial landscapes, and remain curious about the world of finance as you grow your understanding of money and how it can work for you!

Thank you for going on this journey with us. Speak Money is meant to be a guide that you can return to whenever you need to revisit certain topics or need inspiration as you embark on your financial literacy journey. The path to financial literacy is not always straightforward, but with determination and the principles outlined in these pages, you have the tools to conquer financial challenges, seize opportunities, and build the life you want!

For additional resources and online worksheets, visit: www. fulphil.org/class-projects

SPEAK MONEY

The Speak Money Cheat Code

CHAPTER 1: THE BASICS OF FINANCIAL LITERACY

1. Financial literacy is the knowledge necessary to make important financial decisions.
2. Financial literacy is important for creating social mobility and generational wealth.
3. The sooner you begin building financial literacy and putting it to action, the better.
4. Everyone has a different relationship with money and a different definition for their financial success.

CHAPTER 2: CAREERS

1. Social capital refers to the potential that individuals have in being able to secure benefits and invent solutions to problems through membership in social networks.
2. When building social capital, it is not about getting our foot in the door, but rather to make sure that we are already inside the door before it opens again for the right opportunity.

3. Employee benefits include various types of non-wage compensation provided to employees in addition to their normal wages or salaries.
4. The #1 rule is to ALWAYS negotiate.

CHAPTER 3: BUDGETING

1. Budgeting is the process of creating a plan to spend your money.
2. Budgeting is important to help you identify bad spending habits; strategize how to live within your means to work towards your savings goals; control your credit; be prepared for emergencies; and ultimately help you relieve your stress and help you obtain the lifestyle you want.
3. The main components of a budget are your income and expenses.
4. Different budgeting strategies include the zero-based budget, the pay-yourself-first budget, the envelope budget, the 50/30/20 budget, and the "no" budget.

CHAPTER 4: CREATING FINANCIAL STATEMENTS & UNDERSTANDING WEALTH

1. Personal financial statements are methods to help you plan your budget and also set goals for increasing your net worth.
2. The two main types of personal financial statements are: cash flow statements and balance sheets.
3. Net Cash Flow = Cash Inflow - Cash Outflow
4. Net worth = Assets - Liabilities
5. Being wealth is not the same as being rich. Wealthy people have a higher chance at keeping their than rich people do due to:

(1) the ability to grow their assets and (2) the consequences of lifestyle inflation.

CHAPTER 5: DISPARITY & BUILDING WEALTH

1. Generational wealth is any kind of asset that families pass down to their children or grandchildren, whether in the form of cash, investment funds, stocks and bonds, properties, or even entire companies.
2. The generational wealth gap is the difference between the amount of wealth accumulated within one generation, relative to the wealth accumulated within another generation.
3. The racial wealth gap is the disparity in assets of typical households across race and ethnicity. It roots deep in US history and also has systemic influence with our education systems.
4. There are various myths about the racial wealth gap but some solutions that economists predict to have potential to close it include reparations and "Baby Bonds."

CHAPTER 6: SAVINGS & DEBT

1. Savings is the total amount of money that you have remaining after you spend money from your income.
2. Savings rate = Savings / Disposable Income
3. You can grow your savings by increasing your income, cutting down on your expenses, or paying off or refinancing your debt.
4. Debt is the money you owe to another individual or corporation that you borrowed from.

CHAPTER 7: RETIREMENT PLANNING

1. Retirement planning is the process of leveraging financial strategies of saving, investing, and distributing money to sustain yourself during retirement once your paid work ends.
2. Employee benefits are various types of non-wage compensation that employers provide to their employees in addition to their normal wages or salaries.
3. You can leverage plans including Across the Roth IRA, 401(k), and 403(b) to build your retirement savings.

CHAPTER 8: INVESTING

1. Investing is the act of allocating resources, usually money, with the expectation of generating an income or profit.
2. Diversification is an effective investing strategy to lower risk.
3. Different popular types of investment include stocks, bonds, and mutual funds.
4. Index funds are mutual funds that are passively managed.

CHAPTER 9: INSURANCE

1. Insurance is important because risk is unavoidable and can be costly.
2. The Affordable Care Act (ACA) is US healthcare reform law aimed at improving access to health insurance and healthcare.
3. You can pay for insurance through premiums, Explanation of Benefits (EOBS), and Electronic Remittance Advice (ERAs).
4. Life insurance, health insurance, car insurance are some of the most common types of insurance.

CHAPTER 10: TAXES

1. Taxes are a mandatory sum of money that must be paid and is charged by the local, regional, and national arms of government for public purposes.

2. Filing your tax returns is mandatory, and the main components that go into it include your income, deductions, and tax credits. Tax return forms will vary based on the needs of varying individual and organization.

3. Wealthy individuals' taxes are lowered when they invest in assets, pay themselves lower salaries, and rely on loans.

CHAPTER 11: CREDIT

1. Credit is the contractual agreement in which a borrower receives a sum of money or something in value and repays the lender at a later date, generally with interest.

2. Interest rate is defined as an additional charge to the amount you must repay your lender over the time you are borrowing their money. As time passes, your interest adds up, or compounds. This is known as compound interest. Compound interest when you earn interest on the money you save and the money you earn.

3. There are different types of credit including installment credit and revolving credit.

4. You can improve your credit by keeping your credit card balances low; paying your bills on time; paying more than the minimum amount you are asked to pay; considering paying off

higher debt accounts first; not closing accounts unnecessarily; checking your credit reports often; and spending responsibly.

CHAPTER 12: BANKS

1. The main function of banks is facilitating the borrowing and lending process.
2. Common types of banks and systems include retail banking, credit unions, commercial or corporate thinking, and investment banking.
3. The Federal Reserve is the central bank of the United States, and it oversees everything, from managing inflation and regulating all aspects of banking on an international level to managing the supply of US dollars in national circulation.
4. The "unbanked" population refers to individuals who do not have a traditional bank account or access to mainstream financial services due to general distrust in banks.

CHAPTER 13: FINANCIAL LITERACY OF THE FUTURE: WEB 3.0, DECENTRALIZATION, DEFI, & BLOCKCHAIN

1. Web 1.0 was a time of content consumption and reading only. Web 2.0 is a period of interaction, including both reading AND writing. Web 3.0 is the third and most recent generation of the internet, where decentralization allows users to read, write, and own content.
2. Centralization refers to the idea of an entity having total control over an entire platform; decentralization means that a single entity does not have control over all data and processing.

3. Decentralized Finance (DeFi) refers to financial services and applications built on blockchain technology, often removing intermediaries.
4. Blockchain is a decentralized digital ledger that records different transactions in a distributed network.

CHAPTER 14: FINANCIAL LITERACY OF THE FUTURE: MAKING SENSE OF CRYPTOCURRENCY

1. The concept of cryptocurrency is separated into different "layers" to help it operate.
2. Bitcoin is one of the first popularized decentralized digital currencies that can be transferred on a peer-to-peer network.
3. The Blockchain Tri-lemma, essentially suggests that there is a three-way tradeoff that happens between scalability, security, and decentralization.

CHAPTER 15: FINANCIAL LITERACY OF THE FUTURE: BUILDING (MORE) WEALTH IN A WEB 3.0 WORLD

1. Tokenization is the act of converting the value of something into blockchain terms to give you ownership in the Web 3.0 world.
2. Fungible assets are assets that can be replaceable by a similar type of item, which is easier to divide; non-fungible assets are not replaceable.
3. Metaverse is perceived to present potential up-and-coming opportunities for growing wealth.
4. The Dot-Com Boom and Bust can tell us a lot about what is happening with our economy now.

Glossary

CHAPTER 1: THE BASICS OF FINANCIAL LITERACY

Financial literacy: The ability to understand and manage financial concepts and make informed decisions about money.

Emergency fund: A savings fund set aside for unexpected expenses or financial emergencies.

Credit: The ability to borrow money or access goods and services with the promise of repayment in the future.

ROI (Return on Investment): A measure of the profitability or performance of an investment, expressed as a percentage of the initial investment.

CHAPTER 2: CAREERS

Social capital: The network of relationships and connections that can be valuable for career and personal growth.

Retirement fund: A savings account or investment specifically designated for funding one's retirement.

Employee benefits: Perks and advantages provided by an employer to employees in addition to their salary, such as health insurance or retirement plans.

Disability insurance: A type of insurance that provides financial protection in the event of disability or injury preventing an individual from working.

The Family and Medical Leave Act (FMLA): A US federal law that grants eligible employees job-protected unpaid leave for family or medical reasons.

Flea market: A type of open-air space where people to sell or trade a diverse assortment of second-hand goods, vintage items, antiques, collectibles, and handmade products at bargain prices

Negotiation: The process of reaching an agreement through communication and compromise.

CHAPTER 3: BUDGETING

Budgeting: The process of creating a financial plan to allocate income to various expenses and financial goals.

Budget: A detailed plan that outlines income and expenses for a specific period.

Identity capital: Personal attributes, skills, and qualities that contribute to an individual's value in the job market and in life.

Zero-based budget: A budgeting approach where every dollar is allocated to an expense or savings, leaving no money unaccounted for.

Income: Money received regularly, often from employment or investments.

Expenses: Costs associated with various aspects of life, including bills, living expenses, and discretionary spending.

Pay-yourself-first budget: A budgeting method that prioritizes saving or investing a portion of income before paying other expenses.

Envelope system budget: A budgeting technique where cash is divided into envelopes for specific spending categories to help control expenses.

Inflation: The gradual increase in prices and decrease in the purchasing power of money over time.

50/30/20 budgeting: A budgeting rule where 50% of income goes to needs, 30% to wants, and 20% to savings and debt repayment.

The "No" budget: A budgeting approach where unnecessary expenses are minimized or eliminated.

CHAPTER 4: CREATING FINANCIAL STATEMENTS & UNDERSTANDING WEALTH

Personal financial statements: Documents that summarize an individual's financial situation, including assets, liabilities, and net worth.

Cash inflow: Money coming into one's finances, often from sources like employment or investments.

Dividends: Payments received by shareholders from a company's profits.

Capital gains: Profits earned from the sale of assets or investments.

Cash outflow: Money leaving one's finances, typically used for expenses and investments.

Cash flow: The movement of money in and out of an individual's or a business's finances.

Net cash flow: The difference between cash inflow and cash outflow, indicating overall financial health.

Personal Cash Flow Statement: A financial document showing cash inflow and outflow to assess financial stability.

Refinancing: The process of replacing an existing loan with a new one, often to secure better terms.

Personal Balance Sheet: A financial statement that lists an individual's assets and liabilities to determine net worth.

Wealth: The accumulation of assets and financial resources.

Net worth: The difference between an individual's assets and liabilities.

Assets: Valuable possessions or resources that can be converted into cash or used for future benefit.

Liabilities: Financial obligations or debts owed by an individual.

Liquid assets: Assets that can be quickly converted into cash.

Large assets: High-value possessions, such as real estate or expensive vehicles.

Digital assets: Assets stored in digital form, such as cryptocurrencies or online investments.

Investments: Assets purchased with the expectation of generating income or appreciating in value.

Fixed assets: Long-term assets used in the operation of a business, such as machinery or real estate.

Useful life: The approximate amount of time that the asset can help you earn money

Intangible assets: Non-physical assets, such as intellectual property or trademarks.

Tangible assets: Physical assets with monetary value, like real estate or vehicles.

Lifestyle inflation: The tendency to increase spending as income rises, leading to higher expenses.

CHAPTER 5: Disparity & Building Wealth

Generational wealth: Wealth passed down through generations, often in the form of assets or financial resources.

Generational wealth gap: The difference in financial well-being between different generations.

Great Recession: The severe economic downturn that began in 2007 and had a significant impact on the global economy.

Affordable housing crisis: A situation where there is a lack of affordable housing options for a significant portion of the population.

Racial wealth gap: Disparities in wealth between different racial and ethnic groups.

Reconstruction: The period following the American Civil War when efforts were made to rebuild the South and address issues related to race and civil rights.

HBCU (Historically Black College and University): Educational institutions in the United States established primarily for the education of African American students.

Abolition movement: A social and political movement advocating for the abolition of slavery.

Sharecropping: A system of farming in which landless farmers worked on land owned by others in exchange for a share of the crop.

The Freedman Savings Bank: A bank established in the 1860s to provide financial services to newly emancipated African Americans.

"Black Codes": Laws enacted in the post-Civil War South that aimed to restrict the rights and freedom of African Americans.

Jim Crow Laws: Laws that enforced racial segregation and discrimination in the Southern United States.

Fair Housing Administration (FHA): A government agency established to improve housing and homeownership opportunities.

Redlining: A discriminatory practice that involved denying or limiting financial services to certain neighborhoods based on their racial composition.

Upward Mobility: The ability to improve one's socioeconomic status and achieve a higher standard of living.

Poor People's Campaign: A movement advocating for economic and social justice for low-income individuals and communities.

Intergenerational wealth: The transfer of wealth and assets from one generation to the next, often within families.

CHAPTER 6: SAVINGS & DEBT

Savings: Money set aside for future use or unexpected expenses.

Cash equivalents: Highly liquid and low-risk assets that can be quickly converted into cash.

Checking accounts: Bank accounts designed for everyday transactions and payments.

Savings accounts: Bank accounts that offer interest on deposited funds and are typically used for saving.

Money market accounts: Interest-bearing bank accounts that often offer higher interest rates than regular savings accounts.

Certificate of Deposits (CDs): Time-bound savings accounts with higher interest rates, where funds are locked in for a specified period.

Savings rate: The percentage of income that individuals save, often expressed as a savings rate.

Gross margin: The difference between revenue and the cost of goods sold, representing a company's profitability.

Time Value of Money (TVM): The concept that money today is worth more than the same amount in the future due to its potential to earn interest or returns.

Inflation: The gradual increase in prices and decrease in the purchasing power of money over time.

Debt: Money owed to creditors, often with interest.

Snowball Method: A debt repayment strategy that focuses on paying off the smallest debts first.

Debt Avalanche: A debt repayment strategy that focuses on paying off debts with the highest interest rates first.

Debt Consolidation: Combining multiple debts into a single, often lower-interest, loan or repayment plan.

CHAPTER 7: RETIREMENT PLANNING

Retirement planning: The process of preparing for financial security during retirement.

Future expenses: Anticipated financial needs during retirement, such as living expenses and healthcare costs.

Life expectancy: The average number of years a person is expected to live.

Employee benefits: Perks and advantages provided by an employer to employees, including retirement plans.

Roth 401(k): A retirement savings plan that allows contributions with after-tax dollars and tax-free withdrawals in retirement.

Roth 401(b): Similar to a Roth 401(k), but typically offered by nonprofit organizations.

Mutual funds: Investment vehicles that pool money from multiple investors to purchase a diversified portfolio of stocks, bonds, or other securities.

Annuities: Financial products that provide a series of payments at regular intervals, often used for retirement income.

Employer Match: An employer's contribution to an employee's retirement account, often based on the employee's contributions.

Catch-up contribution: Additional contributions allowed for individuals aged 50 and older in retirement accounts.

IRA (Individual Retirement Account): A tax-advantaged account for individuals to save for retirement.

Traditional IRA: An IRA where contributions are often tax-deductible, but withdrawals are taxed.

Tax deferral: The postponement of tax liability to a later date, often in retirement accounts.

Roth IRA: An IRA where contributions are made with after-tax dollars, and withdrawals in retirement are tax-free.

Tax deductible: Expenses or contributions that reduce taxable income, resulting in lower taxes.

CHAPTER 8: Investing

Diversification: Spreading investments across a variety of assets to reduce risk.

Stocks: Ownership shares in a company, representing a claim on its assets and earnings.

Securities: Financial instruments, such as stocks, bonds, and options, that can be bought and sold.

Shares: Units of ownership in a company, often represented by stocks.

Preferred Stock: A type of stock that offers certain privileges, such as fixed dividends.

Common stock: The most common type of stock, representing ownership in a company with voting rights.

Bonds: Debt securities where investors lend money to an entity in exchange for regular interest payments and return of principal.

Fixed Income Security: An investment that pays a fixed amount of interest or dividend at regular intervals.

Default: The failure to meet financial obligations, such as making interest or principal payments on a debt.

Mutual Funds: Investment vehicles that pool funds from multiple investors to invest in a diversified portfolio.

The market: The overall financial marketplace where assets are bought and sold.

Index: A benchmark used to gauge the performance of a group of investments.

Index funds: Mutual funds or exchange-traded funds (ETFs) that aim to replicate the performance of a specific index.

S&P 500: A widely followed stock market index that includes 500 of the largest publicly traded companies in the United States.

CHAPTER 9: Affordable Care Act, Insurance, and Risk Management

Affordable Care Act: A US healthcare reform law aimed at improving access to health insurance and healthcare.

Premium: The cost of health insurance paid by the insured person or their employer.

EOB (Explanation of Benefits): A statement from an insurance company explaining how an insurance claim was processed.

Copay: A fixed amount that an insured person pays for specific medical services.

Electronic Remittance Advice: An electronic statement detailing insurance claim payments and denials.

Term life insurance: Life insurance that provides coverage for a specified term, often with lower premiums.

Whole life insurance: Permanent life insurance that covers the entire lifetime of the insured and includes a cash value component.

Medicare: A US federal health insurance program for people aged 65 and older, as well as some younger individuals with disabilities.

Medicaid: A US federal and state program providing healthcare coverage to eligible low-income individuals and families.

Liability insurance: Coverage that protects the insured from claims and lawsuits resulting from their actions.

Comprehensive coverage: Auto insurance that covers damage to a vehicle from causes other than a collision.

Replacement cost: The cost to replace a damaged or destroyed item with a new one.

Actual Cash Value: The value of an item, taking into account depreciation and wear and tear.

Extended Replacement Cost/Value: Additional coverage that pays for replacement costs beyond the policy's stated limits.

CHAPTER 10: Taxes

Taxes: Mandatory financial contributions to governments used to fund public services and infrastructure.

Tax revenues: The income generated by governments from taxation.

Individual income taxes: Taxes levied on the income of individuals.

Consumption taxes: Taxes applied to the purchase of goods and services.

Tax return: A document filed with a tax authority, reporting income and expenses for tax purposes.

Internal Revenue Service (IRS): The US government agency responsible for collecting taxes and enforcing tax laws.

Form 4868: An IRS form used to request an extension for filing an individual tax return.

Form W-2: A tax form provided by employers to report an employee's earnings and taxes withheld.

Tax Cuts and Job Act (TCJA): US tax reform legislation enacted in 2017, affecting tax rates and deductions.

Standard Tax Deductions: A fixed deduction amount that reduces taxable income without itemizing deductions.

Form 1040-NR: An IRS tax form for nonresident aliens with US income.

Nonresident Aliens: Individuals who are not US citizens or residents for tax purposes.

Form 1040-C: An IRS form for departing aliens to report income and pay taxes before leaving the US

Form 1040-ES: An IRS form for estimating and paying estimated tax for the current year.

Quarter: A three-month period used for financial reporting and tax calculations.

Quarterly taxes: Estimated tax payments made four times a year.

Form 1040-X: An IRS form used to amend a previously filed tax return.

Form 1040-SR: A simplified version of Form 1040 for senior citizens.

Form 1120: An IRS form for corporations to report income and calculate taxes.

LLC (Limited Liability Corporation): A business structure that offers limited liability to its owners while allowing flexibility in management.

Partnerships: Business structures where two or more individuals share ownership and responsibilities.

Form 1065: An IRS form for partnerships to report income and expenses.

Private Mortgage Insurance: Insurance that protects lenders in case of borrower default on a mortgage.

Chapter 11: Credit

Credit: The ability to borrow money or access goods and services with the promise of repayment in the future.

Creditors: Entities that lend money or provide goods or services on credit.

Credit scores: Numeric representations of an individual's creditworthiness, often used by lenders to assess risk.

Creditworthiness: An individual's ability to meet financial obligations based on their credit history.

Credit history: A record of an individual's borrowing and repayment activities.

Credit report: A document summarizing an individual's credit history and financial behavior.

Interest rate: The cost of borrowing money or the return on an investment, expressed as a percentage.

Compound interest: Interest that accrues on both the initial principal and any accumulated interest.

Installment credit: A type of credit where borrowers make regular payments over time, often with a fixed schedule.

Closed-end credit: Credit with a fixed amount, often associated with loans for specific purchases.

Non-revolving credit: Credit that cannot be reused once it's repaid, such as an auto loan.

Origination fees: Charges associated with creating a new loan or credit account.

Discount fees: Reductions in the purchase price or fees applied to a loan, typically for early repayment.

Points: Fees paid to a lender or broker for securing a lower interest rate on a loan.

Late fees: Penalties imposed for missing or making late payments.

Revolving credit: A type of credit with a revolving balance, such as credit cards.

Open credit/Open-ended credit: Credit that can be used repeatedly, like a credit card.

Credit limit: The maximum amount of credit a borrower can access or charge on a credit card.

Home equity line of credit (HELOC): A revolving line of credit that uses a homeowner's equity as collateral.

The Diners Club: One of the first credit card companies, offering charge cards for travel and entertainment expenses.

Closed-loop system: A credit card system that can only be used with specific merchants or at certain locations.

Open-loop system: Credit card systems accepted by a wide range of merchants and locations.

Co-signer: An individual who agrees to share responsibility for a loan or credit with the primary borrower.

Annual Percentage Rate (APR): The annualized interest rate applied to loans and credit cards, including additional fees.

Minimum repayment: The lowest amount a borrower must pay toward their credit card balance each month.

Annual fee: A yearly charge for maintaining a credit card or other financial product.

Charges: Costs associated with credit card usage, such as annual fees or late payment fees.

Interest rates: Rates charged on credit card balances or loans, often based on creditworthiness.

Loyalty points: Rewards offered by credit card companies or retailers for making purchases.

Rewards: Incentives for using a credit card, such as cash back, miles, or merchandise.

Cash back: A credit card reward that provides a percentage of the purchase amount as cash.

Credit utilization ratio: The ratio of credit used to credit available, affecting credit scores.

Revolving utilization: The portion of a credit limit used on a revolving credit account.

Identity theft: Unauthorized use of an individual's personal and financial information for fraudulent purposes.

CHAPTER 12: Banks

Banks: Financial institutions that provide a range of financial services, including deposits, loans, and investment services.

Depositors: Individuals or entities who place money in bank accounts for safekeeping or earning interest.

Wealth management: Services offered by financial institutions to help individuals manage their investments and financial assets.

Assets Under Management (AUM): The total value of assets that a financial institution manages on behalf of clients.

Currency exchange: The process of converting one currency into another for various financial transactions.

Safe deposit boxes: Secure storage containers provided by banks for the safekeeping of valuable items.

Retail banking: Banking services provided to individual consumers, such as checking and savings accounts.

Consumer banking: Banking services designed for personal use, including loans and credit cards.

Unbanked: a population of individuals who do not have a traditional bank account or access to mainstream financial services, such as savings and checking accounts, credit cards, or loans, through a regulated financial institution.

Credit unions: Non-profit financial cooperatives that offer banking services to members.

Commercial or corporate banking: Banking services designed for businesses, including business loans and treasury services.

The Unbanked: Individuals or households without access to traditional banking services.

The Underbanked: Individuals or households with limited access to traditional banking services.

CHAPTER 13: Financial Literacy of the Future: Web 3.0, Decentralization, DEFI, and Blockchain

FinTech: Financial technology, encompassing innovations in the financial industry, including digital banking and payment apps.

Web 1.0: The early stage of the World Wide Web, characterized by static web pages and limited interactivity.

Web 2.0: The phase of the internet marked by dynamic, interactive, and user-generated content.

Web 3.0: The concept of a future web characterized by decentralized and interoperable applications and services.

Centralization: The concentration of control and authority within a single entity or system.

Decentralization: The distribution of control and decision-making across a network of nodes or participants.

Decentralized Finance (DeFi): Financial services and applications built on blockchain technology, often removing intermediaries.

Ledger: A distributed and tamper-proof record of transactions, often associated with blockchain technology.

Mining: The process of validating and adding transactions to a blockchain while securing the network.

Blockchain: A decentralized and immutable digital ledger technology used for recording transactions.

Nodes: Individual devices or computers that participate in a blockchain network.

Smart Contract: Self-executing contracts with the terms of the agreement directly written into code.

CHAPTER 14: Financial literacy of the future: Making sense of cryptocurrency

Layer 0 / Settlement Layer: The foundational layer of a blockchain network responsible for securing transactions.

Layer 1 / Protocol Layer: The layer of a blockchain network that establishes the rules and protocols for transactions.

Bitcoin: The first and most well-known cryptocurrency, created as a digital alternative to traditional currencies.

Cryptocurrency ("Crypto"): Digital or virtual currencies that use cryptography for security and operate on blockchain technology.

Cryptography: Techniques used to secure and protect information, often in the context of cryptocurrency.

Ether/Ethereum (ETH): The cryptocurrency used on the Ethereum blockchain, known for enabling smart contracts.

Layer 2: Secondary layers built on top of a blockchain to improve scalability and reduce fees.

Dogecoin (DOGE): A cryptocurrency initially created as a meme, characterized by a Shiba Inu dog.

Solana: A blockchain platform known for its speed and scalability.

Gas fee: The cost associated with processing transactions on blockchain networks.

Bitcoin Tri-lemma: A concept suggesting that blockchain networks must balance security, decentralization, and scalability.

Throughput: The number of transactions a blockchain can process within a specific time period.

CHAPTER 15: FINANCIAL LITERACY OF THE FUTURE: BUILDING (MORE) WEALTH IN A WEB 3.0 WORLD

Tokenization: The process of converting assets, such as real estate or art, into digital tokens on a blockchain.

Fungible: Items or assets that are interchangeable with others of the same type and value.

Fungible assets: Interchangeable assets, like traditional currencies or commodity tokens.

Non-fungible assets: Unique and non-interchangeable assets, often represented as NFTs.

Non-fungible tokens (NFTs): Digital tokens representing ownership of unique digital or physical items.

Bored Ape Yacht Club: A collection of NFTs featuring cartoon ape art and virtual ownership rights.

Opensea: An online marketplace for trading and owning NFTs.

Metaverse: A digital or virtual world where people can interact, socialize, and conduct business.

Decentraland: A virtual world built on blockchain technology that allows users to create and trade in a virtual environment.

Libra: A cryptocurrency project initially proposed by Facebook (now known as Diem).

Virtual marketplace: An online platform where users can buy and sell virtual assets, goods, or services.

Art galleries: Virtual spaces for displaying and trading digital or NFT-based art.

Sandbox: A virtual or digital environment for testing and experimentation.

Dot-com Boom and Bust: The rapid growth and subsequent crash of internet-related companies in the late 1990s and early 2000s.

Index

1. **#moneytok:** The Economist Newspaper. (2022, January 29). *Personal finance is a hit on TikTok.* The Economist. https://www.economist.com/finance-and-economics/2022/01/29/personal-finance-is-a-hit-on-tiktok

2. **Financial literacy definition:** Fernando, J. (2023, March 30). *Financial literacy: What it is, and why it is so important.* Investopedia. https://www.investopedia.com/terms/f/financial-literacy.asp

3. **Retirement savings statistic:** USAFacts. (2023, April 25). *Half of American households have no retirement savings.* https://usafacts.org/data-projects/retirement-savings

4. **Millennial financial literacy gap:** *Millennials show alarming gap between financial confidence and knowledge.* NEFE. (2017, February 9). https://www.nefe.org/news/2017/02/millennials-show-alarming-gap-between-financial-confidence-and-knowledge.aspx

5. **Millennial financial literacy gap:** Yahoo! (2020, February 25). *New report finds only 16% of millennials qualify as "financially literate."* Yahoo! Finance. https://finance.yahoo.com/news/a-new-report-finds-only-16-of-millennials-qualify-at-financially-literate-195635534.html

6. **Gen Z gap:** Perna, M. C. (2022, October 12). *Why Financial Literacy isn't gen Z's sweet spot-yet.* Forbes. https://www.forbes.com/sites/markcperna/2022/09/13/why-financial-literacy-isnt-gen-zs-sweet-spot-yet/?sh=79ece779627c

7. **Emergency fund:** *Saving for an emergency. How Much Should You Be Saving for an Emergency?* | Wells Fargo. (n.d.). https://www.wellsfargo.com/financial-education/basic-finances/manage-money/cashflow-savings/emergencies/

8. **Credit:** Person. (2022, July 7). *What is credit & how does it work?.* Capital One. https://www.capitalone.com/learn-grow/money-management/what-is-credit/

9. **Rich Dad, Poor Dad:** Kiyosaki, R. T. (2023). *Rich Dad, poor dad.* FBV.

10. **Kiyosaki article**: Team, R. D. P. F. (2011, September 20). *A different financial education (in 17 definitive lessons).* Rich Dad | Financial Education & Coaching for Everyone. https://www.richdad.com/17-financial-education-lessons

11. **Racial wealth gap:** Mollenkamp, D. T. (2023, July 1). *The racial gap in financial literacy.* Investopedia. https://www.investopedia.com/the-racial-gap-in-financial-literacy-5119258

12. **Post-COVID-19 consumer behavior:** Segal, T. (2022, July 5). *How covid-19 changed consumer shopping behavior.* Investopedia. https://www.investopedia.com/how-we-shop-now-5184434

13. **"One-click" shopping:** *Why Amazon's "1-click" ordering was a game changer.* Knowledge at Wharton. (2014, September 14). https://knowledge.wharton.upenn.edu/podcast/knowledge-at-wharton-podcast/amazons-1-click-goes-off-patent/

14. **Predatory lending:** Hayes, A. (2023, May 23). *Predatory lending: How to avoid, examples and protections.* Investopedia. https://www.investopedia.com/terms/p/predatory_lending.asp

15. **Relationship with money:** *Understand your relationship with money.* Wespath Benefits | Investments. (n.d.). https://www.wespath.org/health-well-being/health-well-being-resources/financial-well-being/understand-your-relationship-with-money

16. **Happy Money:** Honda, K. (2020). *Happy money: The Japanese art of making peace with your money.* John Murray Learning.

17. **Social capital:** Kenton, W. (2022, November 27). *What is social capital? definition, types, and examples.* Investopedia. https://www.investopedia.com/terms/s/socialcapital.asp

18. **Side Door College Admissions Scandal:** Admission through the 'side door' - the chronicle of higher education. (n.d.). https://www.chronicle.com/package/admission-through-the-side-door/

19. **Six degrees of separation:** *The science behind Six Degrees.* Harvard Business Review. (2014, August 1). https://hbr.org/2003/02/the-science-behind-six-degrees

20. **Disability insurance:** Kagan, J. (2022, March 14). *Disability income (DI) insurance: What it is and how it works.* Investopedia. https://www.investopedia.com/terms/d/diinsurance.asp

21. **FMLA:** *Family and medical leave (FMLA).* DOL. (n.d.). https://www.dol.gov/general/topic/benefits-leave/fmla

22. **Rise in credit scores post-COVID-19:** Wendel, S. (2021, September 7). *State of credit 2021: Rise in scores despite pandemic*

challenges. Experian Insights. https://www.experian.com/blogs/insights/2021/09/state-of-credit-2021/

23. **Budgeting method:** *5 simple budgeting methods.* LendingTree. (2023, September 22). https://www.lendingtree.com/student/simple-budget/

24. **Identity capital:** Lee, I. (2020, November 25). *Defining and building identity capital for taking the best steps in your life.* Goalcast. https://www.goalcast.com/growth-mindset-identity-capital-how-to-build/

25. **50/30/20 budgeting:** Whiteside, E. (n.d.). *The 50/30/20 budget rule explained with examples.* Investopedia. https://www.investopedia.com/ask/answers/022916/what-502030-budget-rule.asp

26. **Cash inflow:** Medleva, V. (n.d.). *What is cash inflow: Definition and meaning.* What is Cash Inflow: Definition and Meaning | Capital.com. https://capital.com/cash-inflow-definition

27. **Dividends definition:** Hayes, A. (n.d.). *Dividends: Definition in stocks and how payments work.* Investopedia. https://www.investopedia.com/terms/d/dividend.asp

28. **Capital gains definition:** Chen, J. (n.d.). *Capital gains: Definition, rules, taxes, and asset types.* Investopedia. https://www.investopedia.com/terms/c/capitalgain.asp

29. **Cash flow definition:** Hayes, A. (n.d.-a). *Cash flow: What it is, how it works, and how to analyze it.* Investopedia. https://www.investopedia.com/terms/c/cashflow.asp

30. **Cash flow statement:** Hayes, A. (n.d.-a). *Cash flow statement: How to read and understand it.* Investopedia. https://www. investopedia.com/terms/c/cashflowstatement.asp

31. **Lifestyle inflation:** Kenton, W. (n.d.). *Lifestyle inflation: What it is, how it works, example.* Investopedia. https://www.investopedia. com/terms/l/lifestyle-inflation.asp

32. **Federal Reserve net worth reporting:** Changes in US.family finances from 2016 to 2019 - federal reserve board. (n.d.-b). https://www.federalreserve.gov/publications/files/scf20.pdf

33. **Nerd Wallet average net worth:** *The average net worth by age: How does yours compare?.* NerdWallet. (n.d.). https://www. nerdwallet.com/article/finance/average-net-worth-by-age

34. **Millennial dominated workforce:** Hoffower, H. (2020, October 12). *Millennials dominate the US workforce, but they're still 10 times poorer than Boomers.* Business Insider. https://www. businessinsider.com/millennials-versus-boomers-wealth-gap-2020-10

35. **Generational wealth gap:** Hoffower, H. (2020a, October 12). *Millennials dominate the US workforce, but they're still 10 times poorer than Boomers.* Business Insider. https://www.businessinsider. com/millennials-versus-boomers-wealth-gap-2020-10

36. **Millennial wealth gap:** Rosalsky, G. (2021, April 27). *There is growing segregation in millennial wealth.* NPR. https://www. npr.org/sections/money/2021/04/27/990770599/there-is-growing-segregation-in-millennial-wealth

37. **Post-pandemic impact on younger workers:** Hoffower, H. (2020a, May 8). *Younger workers are hit hardest in the coronavirus*

job market, and it spells bad news for millennials and gen Z. Business Insider. https://www.businessinsider.com/millennials-gen-z-laid-off-furloughed-coronavirus-job-market-2020-4

38. **Boomer vs. Millennial generational gap:** Hicks, P. (2022, February 2). *Generational wealth gap: Millennial vs boomer wealth gap.* Trust & Will. https://trustandwill.com/learn/generational-wealth-gap

39. **Bloomberg wealth gap statistic:** Tanzi, A. (2021, October 5). *Gen X sees wealth jump 50% in pandemic.* Bloomberg.com. https://www.bloomberg.com/news/articles/2021-10-05/gen-x-leaves-boomers-trailing-with-50-wealth-jump-in-pandemic

40. **Racial wealth gap:** Hamilton, D., & Darity, W. A. (n.d.). The Political Economy of Education, Financial Literacy, and the Racial Wealth Gap. https://files.stlouisfed.org/files/htdocs/publications/review/2017-02-15/the-political-economy-of-education-financial-literacy-and-the-racial-wealth-gap.pdf?stream=business

41. **Reconstruction:** A&E Television Networks. (2023, April 24). *Reconstruction - Civil War End, changes & act of 1867.* History.com. https://www.history.com/topics/american-civil-war/reconstruction

42. **40 Acres and a Mule:** Brown, D. L. (2021, April 15). *40 acres and a mule: How the first reparations for slavery ended in betrayal.* The Washington Post. https://www.washingtonpost.com/history/2021/04/15/40-acres-mule-slavery-reparations/

43. **Reconstruction citizenship:** *Reconstructing citizenship. National Museum of African American History and Culture.* (2022, August 22).

https://nmaahc.si.edu/explore/exhibitions/reconstruction/
citizenship

44. **History of HBCUs:** *Historically Black Colleges and universities - the development of hbcus, academic and social experiences at hbcus, conclusion.* StateUniversity.com. (n.d.). https://education. stateuniversity.com/pages/2046/Historically-Black-Colleges-Universities.html

45. **Freedman's Savings Bank:** Chatman, A. (n.d.). *Black Americans' rocky relationship with banks can be traced back to an institution that promised wealth but collapsed after just 9 years.* Business Insider. https://www.businessinsider.com/personal-finance/freedmans-bank-collapse-black-americans-wealth-2020-9

46. **Black Codes and Jim Crow Laws:** T*he Black Codes and Jim Crow laws. Education.* (n.d.). https://education.nationalgeographic. org/resource/black-codes-and-jim-crow-laws/

47. **Jim Crow Laws:** *What was Jim Crow.* Jim Crow Museum. (n.d.). https://jimcrowmuseum.ferris.edu/what.htm

48. **Jim Crow Laws:** Lee, T. (2019, August 14). *How America's vast racial wealth gap grew: By plunder.* The New York Times. https://www.nytimes.com/interactive/2019/08/14/magazine/racial-wealth-gap.html?mtrref=www.nytimes.com&assetType=PAY WALL&gwh=C932B69559D5B0474FA341F9FC6D7B92&gwt=pay

49. **Jim Crow Laws:** *Jim Crow laws and racial segregation.* Social Welfare History Project. (2023, September 12). https://socialwelfare.library.vcu.edu/eras/civil-war-reconstruction/jim-crow-laws-andracial-segregation/

50. **Redlining in New America:** *Mapping inequality: Redlining in new deal america.* Bunk. (n.d.). https://www.bunkhistory.org/resources/mapping-inequality-redlining-in-new-deal-america

51. **Lasting effects of Redlining:** *How redlining's racist effects lasted for decades.* Bunk. (n.d.-a). https://www.bunkhistory.org/resources/how-redlinings-racist-effects-lasted-for-decades

52. **Civil Rights Act of 1964:** *The Civil Rights Act of 1964: A long struggle for freedom the segregation era (1900–1939).* Library of Congress. (2014, October 10). https://www.loc.gov/exhibits/civil-rights-act/segregation-era.html

53. **Title VII:** *Title VII and employees' legal rights.* Justia. (2023, October 15). https://www.justia.com/employment/employment-discrimination/title-vii/

54. **Segregation of Black Schools:** *The Achievement Gap in Education: Racial segregation versus segregation by poverty.* Brookings. (2022, March 9). https://www.brookings.edu/articles/the-achievement-gap-in-education-racial-segregation-versus-segregation-by-poverty/

55. **Poor People's Campaign:** *Poor People's campaign.* Poor People's Campaign. (n.d.). https://www.poorpeoplescampaign.org/

56. **Civil Rights Movement:** A&E Television Networks. (n.d.). *Civil Rights Movement: Timeline, Key Events & Leaders.* History.com. https://www.history.com/topics/black-history/civil-rights-movement

57. **March on Washington:** *March on Washington for Jobs and Freedom.* The Martin Luther King, Jr. Research and Education Institute.

(n.d.). https://kinginstitute.stanford.edu/march-washington-jobs-and-freedom

58. **Household racial wealth gap:** WP Company. (2020, June 5). *Analysis | the black-white economic divide is as wide as it was in 1968.* The Washington Post. https://www.washingtonpost.com/business/2020/06/04/economic-divide-black-households/

59. **Opportunity Insights, Race:** *Racial disparities.* Opportunity Insights. (2018, November 7). https://opportunityinsights.org/race/

60. **Pew Research Demographic Trends:** *Demographic trends and economic well-being.* (2016, June 27). Pew Research Center's Social & Demographic Trends Project. https://www.pewresearch.org/social-trends/2016/06/27/1-demographic-trends-and-economic-well-being/

61. **Opportunity Atlas:** *The opportunity atlas.* The Opportunity Atlas. (n.d.). https://www.opportunityatlas.org/

62. **New York Times Iteractive White vs. Black Men comparison:** Badger, E., Miller, C. C., Pearce, A., & Quealy, K. (2018, March 19). *Extensive data shows punishing reach of racism for black boys.* The New York Times. https://www.nytimes.com/interactive/2018/03/19/upshot/race-class-white-and-black-men.html

63. **Wealth, not ability, the biggest predictor of future success:** DesRoches, D. (2019, May 16). Georgetown study: Wealth, not ability, the biggest predictor of future success. Connecticut Public. https://www.ctpublic.org/education/2019-05-15/

georgetown-study-wealth-not-ability-the-biggest-predictor-of-future-success

64. **What We Get Wrong About Closing the Racial Wealth Gap:** What we get wrong about closing the racial wealth gap - Duke university. (n.d.-c). https://socialequity.duke.edu/wp-content/uploads/2019/10/what-we-get-wrong.pdf

65. **Reparations:** Darity, W. (2021, September 24). *Why reparations are needed to close the Racial Wealth Gap. The New York Times.* https://www.nytimes.com/2021/09/24/business/reparations-wealth-gap.html

66. **Baby Bonds:** The Samuel Dubois cook center on social equity. (n.d.-c). https://www.socialequity.duke.edu/wp-content/uploads/2019/12/ICCED-Duke_BabyBonds_December2019-Linked.pdf

67. **Japanese Internment Redress:** Qureshi, B. (2013, August 9). *From wrong to right: A US apology for Japanese internment.* NPR. https://www.npr.org/sections/codeswitch/2013/08/09/210138278/japanese-internment-redress

68. **Savings Definition:** Kagan, J. (n.d.). *What are savings? how to calculate your savings rate.* Investopedia. https://www.investopedia.com/terms/s/savings.asp

69. **Cash equivalents:** Chen, J. (n.d.-b). *What are cash equivalents? types, features, examples.* Investopedia. https://www.investopedia.com/terms/c/cashequivalents.asp

70. **Savings Account types:** Lake, R. (2023, September 27). *6 types of savings accounts.* Forbes. https://www.forbes.com/advisor/banking/savings/types-of-savings-accounts/

71. **Savings rate:** Kagan, J. (n.d.-a). *What are savings? how to calculate your savings rate.* Investopedia. https://www.investopedia.com/terms/s/savings.asp

72. **Gross margin:** Bloomenthal, A. (n.d.). *Gross margin: Definition, example, formula, and how to calculate.* Investopedia. https://www.investopedia.com/terms/g/grossmargin.asp

73. **Improving cash flow:** Moskowitz, D. (n.d.). *10 ways to loosen up your cash flow.* Investopedia. https://www.investopedia.com/articles/personal-finance/061215/10-ways-improve-cash-flow.asp

74. **Average US personal savings rate:** *Personal saving rate.* FRED. (2023, September 29). https://fred.stlouisfed.org/series/PSAVERT

75. **Time value of money:** Fernando, J. (n.d.). *Time value of money explained with formula and examples.* Investopedia. https://www.investopedia.com/terms/t/timevalueofmoney.asp

76. **Average American debt by age:** DeMatteo, M. (2023, May 23). *The average American has $90,460 in debt-here's how much debt Americans have at every age.* CNBC. https://www.cnbc.com/select/average-american-debt-by-age/

77. **Debt repayment strategies:** *How to pay off debt faster.* How to Pay Off Debt Faster – Wells Fargo. (n.d.). https://www.wellsfargo.com/goals-credit/smarter-credit/manage-your-debt/pay-off-debt-faster/

78. **Debt Avalanche, Debt Snowball:** Eneriz, A. (n.d.). *Debt avalanche vs. Debt Snowball: What's the difference?* Investopedia. https://

www.investopedia.com/articles/personal-finance/080716/ debt-avalanche-vs-debt-snowball-which-best-you.asp

79. **Retirement planning:** Kagan, J. (n.d.-c). *What is retirement planning? steps, stages, and what to consider.* Investopedia. https:// www.investopedia.com/terms/r/retirement-planning.asp

80. **IRS retirement plans:** *Retirement plans faqs regarding 403(b) tax-sheltered annuity plans.* Internal Revenue Service. (n.d.). https://www.irs.gov/retirement-plans/retirement-plans-faqs-regarding-403b-tax-sheltered-annuity-plans

81. **401(k) and 403(b):** Team, T. I. (n.d.). *401(k) and 403(b) plans: What's the difference?* Investopedia. https://www.investopedia. com/ask/answers/100314/what-difference-between-401k-plan-and-403b-plan.asp

82. **Investing definition:** Picardo, E. (n.d.). *Investing explained: Types of investments and how to get started.* Investopedia. https://www. investopedia.com/terms/i/investing.asp

83. **Diversification definition:** Segal, T. (n.d.). *What is diversification? definition as investing strategy.* Investopedia. https://www. investopedia.com/terms/d/diversification.asp

84. **Stocks:** Hayes, A. (n.d.-d). *Stocks: What they are, main types, how they differ from bonds.* Investopedia. https://www.investopedia. com/terms/s/stock.asp

85. **Bonds:** Fernando, J. (n.d.-a). *Bond: Financial meaning with examples and how they are priced.* Investopedia. https://www. investopedia.com/terms/b/bond.asp

86. **Mutual funds:** Hayes, A. (n.d.-d). *Mutual funds: Different types and how they are priced.* Investopedia. https://www. investopedia.com/terms/m/mutualfund.asp

87. **90% investment professionals can't beat the market:** Rosenberg, E. (n.d.). *Most investment pros can't beat the stock market, so why do everyday investors think they can win?* Business Insider. https:// www.businessinsider.com/personal-finance/investment-pros-cant-beat-the-stock-market-2020-7

88. **Warren Buffet investing advice:** CNBC. (2020, May 4). *Warren Buffett: For most people, the best thing is to do is owning the S&P 500 index fund.* CNBC. https://www.cnbc.com/video/2020/05/04/warren-buffett-investing-advice.html

89. **Forbes best S&P 500:** Reeves, J. (2023, September 27). *5 best S&P 500 index funds of October 2023.* Forbes. https://www.forbes.com/advisor/investing/best-sp-500-index-funds/

90. **Code of Hammurabi and insurance:** Beattie, A. (n.d.). *The history of Insurance.* Investopedia. https://www.investopedia.com/articles/08/history-of-insurance.asp

91. **Healthcare insurance:** *Health coverage protects you from high medical costs.* Health coverage protects you from high medical costs | HealthCare.gov. (n.d.). https://www.healthcare.gov/why-coverage-is-important/protection-from-high-medical-costs/

92. **Motor vehicle safety data:** *Motor Vehicle Safety Data. Motor Vehicle Safety Data | Bureau of Transportation Statistics.* (n.d.). https://www.bts.gov/content/motor-vehicle-safety-data

93. **Motor vehicle costs:** *Costs of motor-vehicle crashes.* Injury Facts. (2023, April 12). https://injuryfacts.nsc.org/all-injuries/costs/guide-to-calculating-costs/data-details/

94. **Ambulance cost:** Pifer, R. (2022, February 22). *Ground ambulance costs continue to soar, study finds. Healthcare Dive.* https://www.healthcaredive.com/news/ground-ambulance-costs-continue-to-soar-study-finds/619195/

95. **Affordable Care Act:** *Affordable care act (ACA) - glossary.* Glossary | HealthCare.gov. (n.d.). https://www.healthcare.gov/glossary/affordable-care-act/

96. **Women pay more autoinsurance:** George, D. (2021, July 15). *Why women pay more on average than men for auto insurance.* The Motley Fool. https://www.fool.com/the-ascent/insurance/auto/articles/why-women-pay-more-on-average-than-men-for-auto-insurance/

97. **Simpsons insurance:** IMDb.com. (2005, March 20). *"the Simpsons" mobile homer.* IMDb. https://www.imdb.com/title/tt0763035/

98. **Failure to file taxes:** *Failure to file penalty.* Internal Revenue Service. (n.d.-a). https://www.irs.gov/payments/failure-to-file-penalty

99. **33% Americans file taxes last-minute:** *Tax Day 2021: America's biggest procrastinators.* IPX1031. (2022, March 30). https://www.ipx1031.com/americas-biggest-tax-procrastinators-2021/

100. **IRS Form 4868:** Weltman, B. (n.d.). *About form 4868: A 6-month extension to File your tax return.* Investopedia. https://www.

investopedia.com/articles/personal-finance/083115/purpose-irs-form-4868.asp

101. **IRS Form W-2:** Team, T. I. (n.d.-b). *Form W-2 wage and tax statement: What it is and how to read it.* Investopedia. https://www.investopedia.com/terms/w/w2form.asp

102. **IRS Form 1040:** *About schedule A (form 1040), itemized deductions.* Internal Revenue Service. (n.d.-a). https://www.irs.gov/forms-pubs/about-schedule-a-form-1040

103. **Stamp Act and Townshend Acts:** Independence Hall Association. (n.d.). *The townshend acts.* ushistory.org. https://www.ushistory.org/us/9d.asp

104. **Income Tax and the Constitution:** Beattie, A. (n.d.-b). Which amendment made income tax legal?. Investopedia. https://www.investopedia.com/ask/answers/09/income-tax-constitutional.asp

105. **TCJA Tax Law:** Fontinelle, A. (n.d.). *How the TCJA tax law affects your personal finances.* Investopedia. https://www.investopedia.com/taxes/how-gop-tax-bill-affects-you/

106. **Nonresident alien:** Block, H. (2023, January 10). *What is a nonresident alien?.* H&R Block®. https://www.hrblock.com/expat-tax-preparation/resource-center/filing/status/what-is-a-nonresident-alien/

107. **Corporation:** Team, T. I. (n.d.-b). *Corporation: What it is and how to form one.* Investopedia. https://www.investopedia.com/terms/c/corporation.asp

108. **Trump $750 Tax:** Jackson, D., & Subramanian, C. (2020, September 29). *Trump says he still can't share returns after report he*

paid only $750 in income taxes in 2016 and 2017. USA Today. https://www.usatoday.com/story/news/politics/2020/09/27/donald-trump-denies-income-tax-report/3556287001/

109. **$1 salary CEOs:** Morrell, A. (2014, April 1). *Facebook's Mark Zuckerberg now among billionaire CEOS earning $1 salary.* Forbes. https://www.forbes.com/sites/alexmorrell/2014/04/01/facebooks-mark-zuckerberg-now-among-billionaire-ceos-earning-1-salary/

110. **Taxing wealth vs. income:** Schneider, H. (2019, October 17). *Explainer: Democrats Warren and Sanders want wealth tax; economists explain how it works.* Reuters. https://www.reuters.com/article/us-usa-economy-wealth-explainer/explainer-democrats-warren-and-sanders-want-wealth-tax-economists-explain-how-it-works-idUSKBN1WW1GZ

111. **Reducing your taxes:** 22 legal secrets to reducing your taxes | personal finance - US news. (n.d.-a). https://money.usnews.com/money/personal-finance/articles/legal-secrets-to-reducing-your-taxes

112. **Influence of credit score:** Axelton, K. (2023, September 26). *How does your credit score affect your interest rate?.* Experian. https://www.experian.com/blogs/ask-experian/why-do-people-with-higher-credit-scores-get-lower-interest-rates/#:~:text=Because%20lenders%20can%20be%20more,with%20a%20high%20interest%20rate.

113. **Benefits of good credit:** VanSomeren, L. (2023, September 7). *9 benefits of good credit and how it can help you financially.* Forbes.

https://www.forbes.com/advisor/credit-score/benefits-of-good-credit/

114. **Installment credit:** McGurran, B. (2023, May 15). *What is installment credit?*. Experian. https://www.experian.com/blogs/ask-experian/what-is-installment-credit/

115. **Origination fee:** Kopp, C. M. (n.d.). *Origination fee: Definition, average cost, and ways to save.* Investopedia. https://www.investopedia.com/terms/o/origination-fee.asp

116. **Open-end credit:** Bankrate. (n.d.). *The difference between revolving and nonrevolving credit.* https://www.bankrate.com/personal-finance/credit/revolving-vs-nonrevolving-credit/

117. **History of credit cards:** *The history of credit cards.* CreditCards.com. (2023, May 8). https://www.creditcards.com/statistics/history-of-credit-cards/

118. **Visa and Mastercard:** Hayes, A. (n.d.-f). *Visa vs. Mastercard: What's the difference?* Investopedia. https://www.investopedia.com/articles/personal-finance/020215/visa-vs-mastercard-there-difference.asp

119. **Fair Debt Collection practices:** Kenton, W. (n.d.-a). *Fair debt collection practices act (FDCPA): Definition and rules.* Investopedia. https://www.investopedia.com/terms/f/fair-debt-collection-practices-act-fdcpa.asp

120. **18 years old to apply for credit card:** Crail, C. (2023, May 15). *How old do you have to be to get a credit card?*. Forbes. https://www.forbes.com/advisor/credit-cards/how-old-do-you-have-to-be-to-get-a-credit-card/

121. **Choosing and applying for a credit card:** *Choosing and applying for a credit card.* Citizens Advice. (n.d.). https://www. citizensadvice.org.uk/debt-and-money/borrowing-money/ credit-cards/choosing-and-applying-for-a-credit-card/

122. **Reasons to say no to credit card:** Fontinelle, A. (n.d.-a). *9 reasons to say no to credit.* Investopedia. https://www.investopedia. com/articles/younginvestors/08/purchase-financing.asp

123. **Roles of banks:** *Jeanne Gobat is a Senior Economist in the IMF's Monetary and Capital Markets Department.* (2017, June 15). Banks: At the heart of the matter. IMF. https://www.imf.org/en/ Publications/fandd/issues/Series/Back-to-Basics/Banks

124. **Retail banking:** Majaski, C. (n.d.). *Retail banking: What it is, different types, and common services.* Investopedia. https://www. investopedia.com/terms/r/retailbanking.asp

125. **Federal Reserve education:** Federal Reserve Education. (n.d.). https://www.federalreserveeducation.org/

126. **FDIC survey:** *Economic inclusion.* FDIC. (n.d.). https://www. fdic.gov/resources/consumers/economic-inclusion/index. html

127. **Predatory lending:** Hayes, A. (2023, May 23). *Predatory lending: How to avoid, examples and protections.* Investopedia. https:// www.investopedia.com/terms/p/predatory_lending.asp

128. **Unbanked prefer alternative cards:** Banking on prepaid report - the pew charitable trusts. (n.d.-c). https://www.pewtrusts. org/~/media/assets/2015/06/bankingonprepaidreport.pdf

129. **Overdraft fees:** Stein, G. (2016, February 25). *New insights on bank overdraft fees and 4 ways to avoid them.* Consumer Financial

Protection Bureau. https://www.consumerfinance.gov/about-us/blog/new-insights-on-bank-overdraft-fees-and-4-ways-to-avoid-them/

130. **How the Other Half Banks:** Baradaran, M. (2018). *How the other half banks: Exclusion, exploitation, and the threat to democracy.* Harvard University Press.

131. **Unbanked:** LaMagna, M. (2016, September 23). *10 million US families don't use a bank - here's what it costs them.* MarketWatch. https://www.marketwatch.com/story/10-million-us-families-dont-use-a-bank-heres-what-it-costs-them-2016-09-23

132. **Web 3.0 definition:** Essex, D., Kerner, S. M., & Gillis, A. S. (2023, September 9). *What is web 3.0 (WEB3)? definition, guide and history.* WhatIs.com. https://www.techtarget.com/whatis/definition/Web-30

133. **Web 1.0, 2.0, 3.0 comparison:** GeeksforGeeks. (2023a, July 2). *Difference between web 1.0, web 2.0, and web 3.0.* GeeksforGeeks. https://www.geeksforgeeks.org/web-1-0-web-2-0-and-web-3-0-with-their-difference/

134. **Coinbase chart:** Coinbase. (n.d.). *A simple guide to the web3 stack.* Coinbase. https://www.coinbase.com/learn/market-updates/around-the-block-issue-22

135. **Meaning of decentralization:** Buterin, V. (2017, February 6). *The meaning of decentralization.* Medium. https://medium.com/@VitalikButerin/the-meaning-of-decentralization-a0c92b76a274

136. **Blockchain:** *WTF is the blockchain?.* HackerNoon. (n.d.). https://hackernoon.com/wtf-is-the-blockchain-1da89ba19348

137. **Ledger**: Merriam-Webster. (n.d.). Ledger definition & meaning. Merriam-Webster. https://www.merriam-webster.com/dictionary/ledger

138. **Unbanked and DeFi:** Cointelegraph. (n.d.). *Banking the unbanked: How defi can help the low-income population.* Cointelegraph. https://cointelegraph.com/learn/banking-the-unbanked-how-defi-can-help-the-low-income-population

139. **Impact of DeFi:** Maksimenka, I. (2021, January 31). *Defi is the future of banking that humanity deserves.* Cointelegraph. https://cointelegraph.com/news/defi-is-the-future-of-banking-that-humanity-deserves

140. **Layer 0:** Binance Academy. (2023, July 4). *What is layer 0 in Blockchain?* https://academy.binance.com/en/articles/what-is-layer-0-in-blockchain

141. **Bitcoin:** Reiff, N. (n.d.). *Bitcoin vs. Ethereum: What's the difference?* Investopedia. https://www.investopedia.com/articles/investing/031416/bitcoin-vs-ethereum-driven-different-purposes.asp

142. **Santoshi Nakamoto Bitcoin paper:** Nakamoto, S. (2008). Bitcoin: A peer-to-peer electronic cash system. Decentralized business review.

143. **Ethereum:** Frankenfield, J. (n.d.). *What is ethereum and how does it work?.* Investopedia. https://www.investopedia.com/terms/e/ethereum.asp

144. **How Dogecoin became so popular:** Leech, O. (2021, September 14). *How dogecoin became so popular.* CoinDesk Latest Headlines

RSS. https://www.coindesk.com/markets/2021/02/16/how-dogecoin-became-so-popular/

145. **Litecoin:** Napoletano, E. (2023, September 22). *What is Litecoin? how does it work?.* Forbes. https://www.forbes.com/advisor/investing/cryptocurrency/litecoin/

146. **Unsustainable mining:** Fontao, A. (2021, November 3). *Environmental impacts of cryptocurrency: A different kind of "mining."* The Daily Californian. https://www.dailycal.org/2021/11/03/environmental-impacts-of-cryptocurrency-a-different-kind-of-mining

147. **Blockchain Trilemma:** Musharraf, M. (2023, July 22). *What is the blockchain trilemma?.* Ledger. https://www.ledger.com/academy/what-is-the-blockchain-trilemma

148. **Metaverse:** Abrol, A. (2023, September 27). *Web 3.0 vs. metaverse: A detailed comparison [updated].* Blockchain Council. https://www.blockchain-council.org/metaverse/web-3-0-vs-metaverse/#:~:text=Metaverse%20technology%20is%20a%20core,rather%20than%20a%20single%20entity

149. **NFTs:** Clark, M. (2021, March 3). *NFTs, explained.* The Verge. https://www.theverge.com/22310188/nft-explainer-what-is-blockchain-crypto-art-faq

150. **Virtual marketplace:** Fonarov, O. (2022, October 12). Council post: *What is the role of nfts in the metaverse?.* Forbes. https://www.forbes.com/sites/forbestechcouncil/2022/03/11/what-is-the-role-of-nfts-in-the-metaverse/?sh=62f734f36bb8

151. **Metaverse Virtual Real Estate:** Mileva, G. (2022, May 4). The Ultimate Guide to Metaverse Virtual Real Estate. Influencer

Marketing Hub. https://influencermarketinghub.com/metaverse-virtual-real-estate/

152. **Metaverse real-estate boom:** YouTube. (2021). *Get Ready for the 2022 Metaverse Real Estate Boom.* YouTube. Retrieved October 16, 2023, from https://www.youtube.com/watch?v=9l08sF5VRAQ.

153. **Virtual Real Estate investing tips:** Mileva, G. (2022a, May 4). How to invest in Virtual Real Estate (Metaverse Real Estate Guide). Influencer Marketing Hub. https://influencermarketinghub.com/metaverse-real-estate/

154. **Dot-com boom and Web 3.0 economy:** Brown, J. (2021, December 10). *The secret to investing in 2021? look to the 2000 dot-com bubble.* Forbes. https://www.forbes.com/sites/investor/2021/02/11/the-secret-to-investing-in-2021-look-to-the-2000-dot-com-bubble/

www.ingramcontent.com/pod-product-compliance
Lightning Source LLC
Chambersburg PA
CBHW071545210326
41597CB00019B/3127